ABOUT THE COVER

The cover illustration represents the coming together in peace of two cultures, the Native American and the French. The Native American is holding a calumet, sometimes called a peace pipe. It was constructed of a hollow reed with or without a pipe bowl and adorned with an eagle feather fan attached at its base. Europeans quickly learned that when a Native American showed a calumet, it was a sign of peaceful intentions. It was a ritual similar in spirit to the exchange of a handshake when one European met another. In the illustration, the calumet is raised to the sky in prayer as the smoke from the burning tobacco inside the reed rises. In the Native American belief system, tobacco smoke was thought to have the power to connect man to the spirit world. The gesture asks for blessings from the spirit world.

The Native American and French coureurs-de-bois, or trappers, established a mutually beneficial trading partnership throughout the Canadian and Louisiana Territories. The white line in the background symbolizes the great river system within the interior of the continent used to move trade goods by flatboats or canoes to and from New Orleans or Quebec. The Missouri and Mississippi rivers were some of the most important highways in this system and the location of St. Louis was carefully chosen to be near the confluence of these great rivers.

The other curved lines represent the rolling hills and river valleys of the area, home to the tribes native to Missouri.

Under Three Flags

Note to Readers

This book is by no means a comprehensive history of St. Louis. Instead it is my account of the early events that shaped our city. I believe the story that follows will help children to understand and appreciate the significance of St. Louis in our history.

ACKNOWLEDGMENTS

I would like to extend my sincere thanks to many people for their assistance in creating this book. The following people have taken time from their busy schedules to provide pertinent information and/or assistance in the taking of on-site photographs: Nancy Smith, John Biermann, Ken Cole of Mastodon State Historic Site; William R. Iseminger, Assistant Site Manager of Cahokia Mounds State Historic Site; Andrew Cooperman of the Cahokia Court House State Historic Site; Kathyn RedCorn, Director, Osage Tribal Museum, Pawhuska, Oklahoma; Richard Owings of St. Louis County Parks Museum of Transportation; Walter Strosnider, who resides on top of Sugar Loaf Mound.

I am deeply grateful to those who read the first drafts and gave me valuable feedback and continual support and encouragement: My family, Marilyn and Charles Hoessle, Tracy and Joel Malke, Brad and Hillary Hoessle, Gabrielle and Kirk Hoessle, and Brad Michaels; various colleagues at Community School, but especially my team teacher, Katie Dolan; and my book club with no name, but who are great friends and avid readers and dancers. I give deep appreciation to David Greenburg and Patricia Hermes, fine children's book authors, who shared their knowledge and inspiration on writing and publishing. Finally, I am greatly indebted to those whose creative talent and foresight made it all possible: Kim Mulkey Young, illustrator and graphic designer; Bryan S. Young, photographer; Fran Levy and Julie Stevenson, editors; Eric Winters, production director; and especially to Jeff Fister, publisher, for his faith in the work and for taking a risk and publishing his first children's book.

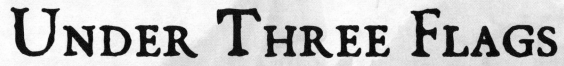

UNDER THREE FLAGS

EXPLORING EARLY ST. LOUIS HISTORY

From The Ice Age To The Louisiana Purchase

WRITTEN BY

MAUREEN HOESSLE

DESIGNED AND ILLUSTRATED BY

KIM MULKEY YOUNG

VIRGINIA PUBLISHING • ST. LOUIS

Under Three Flags
©2005 Maureen Hoessle

Virginia Publishing
P.O. Box 4538
St. Louis, MO 63108
www.STLbooks.com

Illustration and design
©2005
Kim Mulkey Young

Printed in the United
States
*Library of Congress
Control Number:
2004111506*

ISBN: 1-891442-28-7

wild turkey

dried corn

Clovis spear tip

ST. LOUIS

giant sloth

squashes

chunkey player figurine

Pierre Laclède

American buffalo

CONTENTS

beaver

Old Cathedral

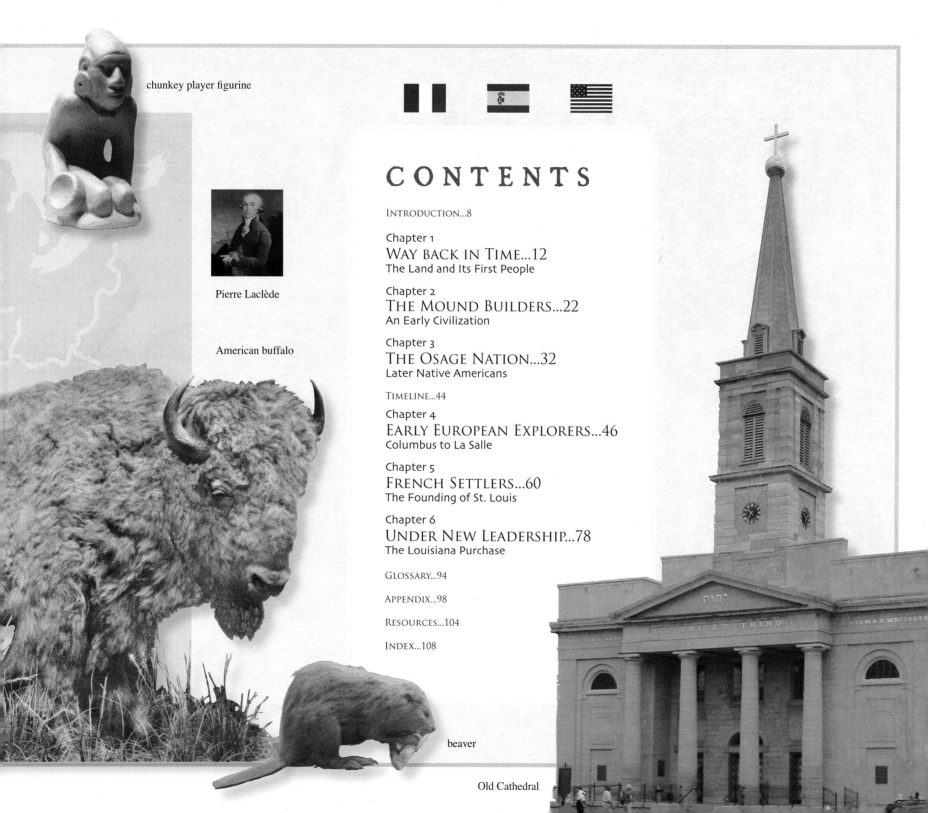

Symbols of St. Louis

The statue of St. Louis stands in front of the Art Museum

The flag of St. Louis shows the confluence of rivers. The fleur-de-lis represents the city's French origins

The Gateway Arch rises on the bank of the Mississippi River

The seal of St. Louis shows a riverboat

Introduction To St. Louis

St. Louis is a modern city with much to offer. It is home to the 630-foot Gateway Arch, which greets travelers and residents alike. Grand skyscrapers of rich architectural design form the riverfront skyline. Lush green parks provide a getaway from the hustle and bustle of busy city life. The zoo and museums of art, science, and history are available free of charge. Baseball, football, and hockey fans enjoy these sports in St. Louis. The Symphony Orchestra and many theater companies perform throughout the year. Today, St. Louis residents come from many **ethnic** backgrounds and share their **cultural heritage** through their foods, art, dance, and daily life in the city's diverse neighborhoods.

In The Beginning

St. Louis is a city with a remarkable history. Hunters of mastodons and giant sloths roamed this area about 12,000 years ago. A people called the "Mound Builders" once formed a great city for thousands and built enormous earthen mounds in this area. Native Americans hunted buffalo and developed a deep relationship with nature and their environment. Three hundred years ago, men from a country across the Atlantic Ocean called France came to explore and claimed the land. Later settlers brought enslaved people of African descent.

The Mississippi River is part of the great water highway on the North American continent. Before there were planes, before there were trains, before there were cars, there were the rivers. Living on a vast continent covered in dense forest, Native

Americans paddled the **network** of rivers in canoes to carry trade goods to distant tribes. The French chose to build St. Louis on the west bank of the Mississippi River and, from the beginning, it has been a river city. Its history and **prosperity** were influenced by its location near the confluence of the Mississippi and Missouri Rivers. Later, St. Louis sat on the edge of the frontier and gave services and supplies to pioneers seeking to explore and settle the vast unexplored continent to the west. This city was at one time where the West began.

Have you ever wondered:

- Who were the first people to live in this area?
- Why did people settle here?
- Why the name "Saint Louis?"
- What did every French child learn to do?
- What were some of the unique things discovered here?
- Why did the flag flying over St. Louis change three times in one day?

TAKE A JOURNEY

As you read this book, you are invited to journey back in time. Imagine a time when there were no bicycles, skateboards, automobiles, televisions, computers, or video games. There were no stoves, refrigerators, air conditioners, telephones, or even bathrooms... no modern conveniences. There were no schools, either.

Nicknames

St. Louis has had many nicknames throughout its history: "Queen of the West," "Lion of the Valley," "The River City," and "Gateway to the West." An early nickname given to St. Louis was "Mound City." Huge earthen mounds built long ago by Native people surrounded the site on which the village of St. Louis was built.

Pain Court

In the first year of the village, the settlers were more interested in trading for furs than farming. They had little time to cultivate the prairies and no wheat was grown. No mill was built to ground the wheat into flour. The settlers went without bread. The French imported supplies from other settlements. This is when St. Louis earned the nickname "Pain Court," meaning "shortage of bread." After that, the settlers made sure there was plenty to eat.

Imagine you are a Native American child fishing in the stream. All of a sudden you spot people with light-colored skin wearing lots of clothes even though it is summer. They speak an unfamiliar language, smell peculiar, and have hairy faces. They carry sticks that spurt smoke, make loud noises, and kill animals. They ride upon the backs of four-legged creatures much larger than dogs.

Imagine you are a European child who took a three-month-long journey across the rough Atlantic Ocean to start a new life in a new world. Escaping crowded and diseased conditions of your home town, you now travel by foot across unknown land and cross raging rivers on rafts in search of the land your family can settle and call your own. You hear about bear attacks and strange people with darker skin.

Imagine you are living the life of an enslaved child. You work from sunrise to sunset six days a week. You are told when to eat, when to rest, when you may have a drink of water. You eat what is provided, often leftover scraps from your owners' meals. You live in a small cabin crowded with your family and perhaps other slaves. Every second of every day you yearn to be free.

Follow in the footsteps of Asians, Africans, and Europeans from distant lands as they cross great land masses, dangerous oceans, and wild rivers to make a home in this place we now call St. Louis.

Enjoy the journey!

EXPLORING THE ST. LOUIS AREA

Reading this book is only part of the adventure. You are invited to go on field trips to explore various sites and learn more amazing facts about the St. Louis area. Here are some examples: Explore where mastodons, large hairy relatives of the modern-day elephant, were first discovered in Missouri. Climb a 100-foot mound built by early Native Americans. See for yourself the meeting of the great waters of the Missouri and Mississippi rivers. Look for a giant Piasa bird first painted along the bluffs by Native Americans. Go to the Old Courthouse to see a diorama of the Day of Three Flags Ceremony.

These are only a few examples of adventures to be had while reading this book. Throughout the chapters, look for the EXPLORE flag. A sample is shown on the side panel side to the right. It will direct you to a museum, park, river, or historical site that will provide not only more information on the history of the area, but fun and entertainment for the whole family. Addresses and phone numbers are listed in the back of this book for quick reference. Take the field trips and enjoy learning even more about the people and events that shaped early St. Louis history.

Words in **bold** are defined in the glossary at the back of the book. If you read an unfamiliar word in a side panel, look in the glossary for its meaning.

Also included at the end of the book are fun facts about what makes St. Louis unique and why it holds an important place in American history.

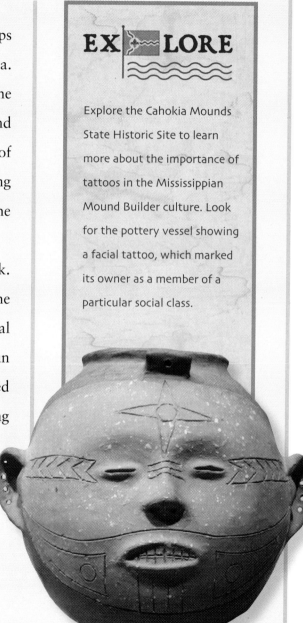

EXPLORE

Explore the Cahokia Mounds State Historic Site to learn more about the importance of tattoos in the Mississippian Mound Builder culture. Look for the pottery vessel showing a facial tattoo, which marked its owner as a member of a particular social class.

ANCIENT BIG GAME HUNTERS

CHAPTER ONE

WAY BACK IN TIME

THE LAND AND ITS FIRST PEOPLE

Our trip begins way back in time, perhaps 30,000 years ago. Imagine living during the end of the Ice Age. You wear clothes your mother makes for you from animal skins and fur that keep you warm in snow and icy weather. Your father carries a spear, one of your family's few possessions. You travel in a small band of people, your extended family, and camp all year long. You are in search of the great mastodon.

Sloth Skins

Evidence suggests that early man used the skin of the giant ground sloth for shelters and other purposes. Dermal ossicles (bone particles that form beneath a sloth's skin during its lifetime) were found at the Kimmswick archeological site near mastodon bones. The discovery of dermal ossicles (shown here actual size) suggests that sloth skins were brought to this site. Perhaps Clovis people also used the sloth skins for camouflage, to conceal their scent when hunting the mastodon.

(This theory is illustrated on page 12.)

GLACIERS AND THE LAND BRIDGE

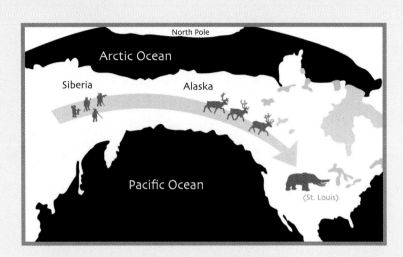

During the **Ice Age**, huge, slow-moving fields of ice called "glaciers" covered much of the northern part of the planet. With so much water frozen, the depth of the seas dropped to about 250 feet. Lower levels exposed a land bridge. This bridge was about 1,000 miles wide and crossed the Bering Sea, connecting today's Asia and North America (near Siberia and Alaska). Many scientists believe that about 30,000 years ago people followed and hunted the large land mammals across this land bridge, now called "Beringia."

When the temperature warmed again, the glaciers melted and sea levels rose. The Ice Age gradually ended. Beringia disappeared beneath the Bering Sea. People had crossed the land bridge for the last time. Over thousands of years, they eventually **migrated** to all parts of North, Central, and South America. They began to change physically and culturally as they **acclimated** to a variety of environments. Over time, a new **classification** of people developed, native to the American continents and distinct from their Asian **ancestors**. These ancient nomadic hunters were the first true Americans.

The first known Native Americans arrived to present-day Missouri about 12,000 years ago. Today archeologists call them "Clovis" people because their stone tools were first discovered in Clovis, New Mexico.

The temperatures shortly after the Ice Age were significantly cooler than they are today. As a result, many of the plants and animals that inhabited the region were different from those found today. The Clovis people arrived in a land covered in forests of spruce and poplar trees and abundant with wildlife. As the temperatures gradually warmed, more ice melted and the environment grew very moist. Ponds, marshes, bogs, and lakes were more plentiful in the area right after the Ice Age.

ANIMALS OF THE LAND

Many animals were enormous back then. There is evidence that people existed at the same time as the huge ancestors of the following animals: bears, wolves, lions, moose, buffalo, beavers, and armadillos. In the area that is now Missouri, however, scientists have proof that only two animals lived at the same time as humans, the mastodon and the giant ground sloth. Mastodons,

THE GIANT
GROUND SLOTH

FLINT KNAPPING

Spear tips, razor-sharp and deadly, were tied to hollow reed shafts with sinew and secured with hide glue.

which were gigantic hairy ancestors of the modern elephant, stood 8 to 10 feet high and had long tusks. Giant ground sloths grew to more than 6 feet tall. Other animals that lived during the time of the Clovis people still exist today: squirrels, woodchucks, rabbits, elk, bison, and white-tailed deer.

THE CLOVIS PEOPLE AND THEIR WAY OF LIFE

The Clovis people were **nomadic** people who followed the herds of animals they hunted. They carried with them their homes, called "hide shelters," made of animal skins. Occasionally the families found caves in which to spend the night. They built campfires for light and heat.

The men hunted with spears tipped with stone blades. The blades were shaped by chipping away flakes of rock called "chert" or "flint" with a rock or bone (a process known as flint knapping). To increase the speed and power of the thrown spear, men used "atlatls." An atlatl enabled the spear to go a much greater distance with stronger force than by hurling the spear by hand. The increased force could penetrate the thick skin of the mastodon.

These early people used many parts of the animals they hunted. Bones were sharpened for use as knives and needles. Portions of the skeleton, antlers and horns

Atlatls were two-foot-long sticks, carved flat and thin. A hunter held one end of the atlatl and placed his spear in a notch at the other end. Then he swung the atlatl overhead while keeping grasp of one end (almost like serving in tennis). This action released and hurled the spear through the air.

were made into tools for skinning hides, butchering meat, and for carving or engraving wood and stone. Mastodon tusks served as frames to support the hide shelters. Skins of animals became clothing and blankets. Sinew, the tough fibrous cord that attaches muscles to the bones, was early woman's thread. People ate meat from the hunt and wild plants and nuts gathered by the women and children.

LARGE ANIMALS DISAPPEAR

The Clovis people followed the mastodon and the giant sloth for thousands of years, but eventually the animals they depended on died out. No one knows for certain why the mastodon and giant sloth disappeared from the earth. Was it the hunting by the Clovis people that caused their **extinction**? These expert hunters may have over-hunted the animals, causing their populations to become smaller and smaller. Mastodon herds consumed great amounts of both water and plant life. Did the climate change from cold and wet to drier and warmer cause ponds to dry up and alter the plant life that the mastodon and giant sloth depended on? Maybe these large mammals died of disease. Did the changing climate expose them to weather for which they were not adapted? Or was it a combination of all these possibilities? No one knows for sure.

EX LORE

Explore the Mastodon State Historic Site to see the location of the dig, a replica of a mastodon skeleton, and a model of a giant sloth. An excellent slide show describes the Ice Age and migration of the people and animals.

The First Horse

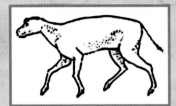

Here's an interesting bit of historic information about the horse. Ancestors of the horse were the size of an average dog. They lived in the Americas during the Ice Age and traveled across the Beringia Land Bridge to Asia. These early horses continued to grow larger as they traveled to Europe and Africa. The horse ancestors that remained in America became extinct. Later, the Spanish brought the horse we know today to the Americas.

PREHISTORIC DISCOVERY

Our story started long before people lived in the Americas. In fact, the continents were not yet known as the Americas. The first people coming to this land had no written language. How do we know what happened in the times before written language, which scientists called **prehistoric** times? We learn from archeologists, scientists who study the **cultures** and lifestyles of ancient people. Archeologists dig into the ground to uncover the remains of people, along with their tools, articles of clothing, pottery, and other **artifacts** long buried. The remains of animals near their camps or villages tell us about the animals they hunted. By studying the layers of soil and rock, archaeologists can determine when and where the people and animals lived. We also learn from oral history – that is, stories passed down from generation to generation.

Even today, archaeologists continue to learn more about the first Americans. New **technologies** allow archeologists to examine the remains of prehistoric cultures in differents ways. These technologies may reveal additional information, and scientists may eventually revise many current conclusions. This book tells the stories of the people of this area as we understand them today.

CONNECTION TO ST. LOUIS

The first evidence that Clovis people hunted the mastodon was discovered in 1979. This occurred in Kimmswick, Missouri, 20 miles south of St. Louis. Dr. Russell Graham from the Illinois State Museum supervised the **excavation** at the site. As a paleontologist (a scientist who studies ancient animal fossils) he was looking for plant and animal remains. Imagine his excitement when he discovered a fluted spear blade touching mastodon bone fragments, proving that people and mastodons existed at the same time, and that the Clovis people hunted mastodon! The photograph of Dr. Graham captures the moment of discovery.

Clovis Spear Tip

This is the Clovis spear tip, actual size shown, discovered at the Kimmswick site. The large size of the tip suggests that it had been newly made.

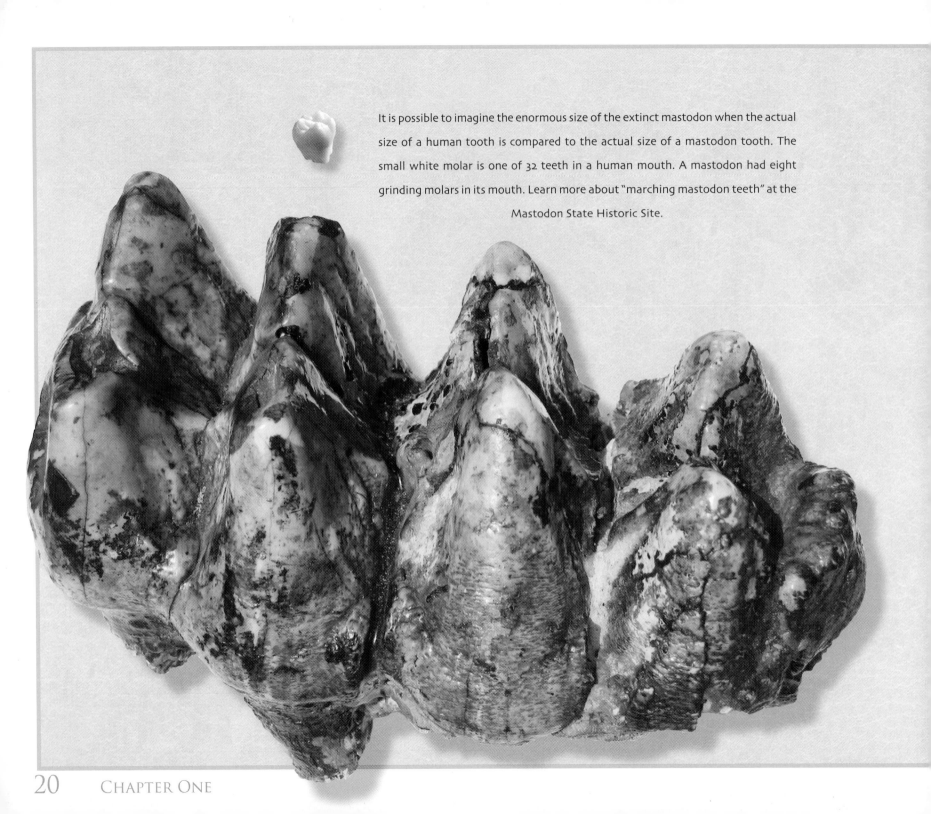

It is possible to imagine the enormous size of the extinct mastodon when the actual size of a human tooth is compared to the actual size of a mastodon tooth. The small white molar is one of 32 teeth in a human mouth. A mastodon had eight grinding molars in its mouth. Learn more about "marching mastodon teeth" at the Mastodon State Historic Site.

Marty meets a mastodon. The mastodon shows her its molars.

TRADING CORN FOR SHELLS

CHAPTER TWO

THE MOUND BUILDERS

AN EARLY CIVILIZATION

Imagine you live in a city built among huge earthen mounds. You watch your father pack his canoe with baskets of dried corn. He paddles for days to distant lands, to distant tribes, to trade the corn grown by your community for precious seashells. When he returns home, your father gives a shell necklace to your chief, the Brother of the Sun. This gift raises your family's **status** in the city.

The Last Mound in St. Louis

More than 25 mounds were located in St. Louis. That is why St. Louis was called "Mound City" in the early 1800s. The mounds were destroyed to build the city. One mound still stands in St. Louis and can be seen from Highway 55 near the 4500 block of Broadway. It was thought to be used as a signal mound for Cahokia. The early French settlers named it "Sugar Loaf" because its shape reminded them of a cake of brown sugar. See if you can find it.

Our story continues among the Mound Builders. Early Native Americans began to settle in communities or villages on both sides of the Mississippi River, in the area that is now **metropolitan** St. Louis. Because it was prehistoric time, we don't know what these people called themselves. Today we call the people who lived here about 3,000 years ago "Mound Builders," because they built giant dirt hills called "mounds." The creation of these mounds took years and required the work of many people, much like the pyramids in Egypt.

The later Mound Builders of this area are called "Mississippians" because they settled in the rich Mississippi River Valley. The Mississippians lived about 1,000 years ago (approximately 700 to 1400 C.E.). Because of a structured social system and the **cultivation** and trading of corn grown in abundance, they developed the largest and most complex prehistoric **civilization** on the American continent north of Mexico.

THE MOUNDS

Around 1200 C.E., the Mississippian Mound Builders in this area organized the mound city now called "Cahokia," which was the religious and ceremonial center for the people of the Mississippi Valley. It is estimated that at one time more than 20,000 people lived within the limits of the city, which was located just 10 miles from present-day downtown St. Louis. Another 20,000 people lived in outlying villages, one of which is now St. Louis.

The Mississippians built mounds in three different shapes.

Cone-shaped mounds were used for **forts** and burial sites.

The ridge-shaped mounds were boundary markers.

Religious ceremonies were held on the immense, flat-topped mounds, where the chief and his family lived. The largest mound, 14 acres and the height of a 10-story building, was built with 22 million cubic feet of dirt!

Organized, cooperative teamwork was needed to build the complex structures of the mounds. Thousands of men dug the earth using hoes made of sticks and stone blades. They loosened dirt and scooped it into baskets with mussel shells. They carried the dirt on their backs, in baskets strapped to their heads, to the nearby mound site. The Mound Builders carefully layered different types of earth as they constructed the mounds to allow for drainage. Eventually, more than 120 mounds were built in the area.

The pits created by the digging were called "borrow pits." Some were filled with water and used for fishing ponds. Other pits were used for trash. Once filled with trash, pits were covered with dirt and the land was reused.

For many generations, over hundreds of years, the Mississippians continu-

(continued on page 27)

Playing Chunkey

Chunkey was a favorite game among men and women. Play began when a player rolled a stone disc across the field. The contestants threw spears trying to mark the spot where the chunkey stone would come to rest. Players sometimes raced along after a throw, using gestures to try to guide the path of the spear. The fans bet on whose spear came the closest when the stone landed and cheered the winner. The game was played all day long.

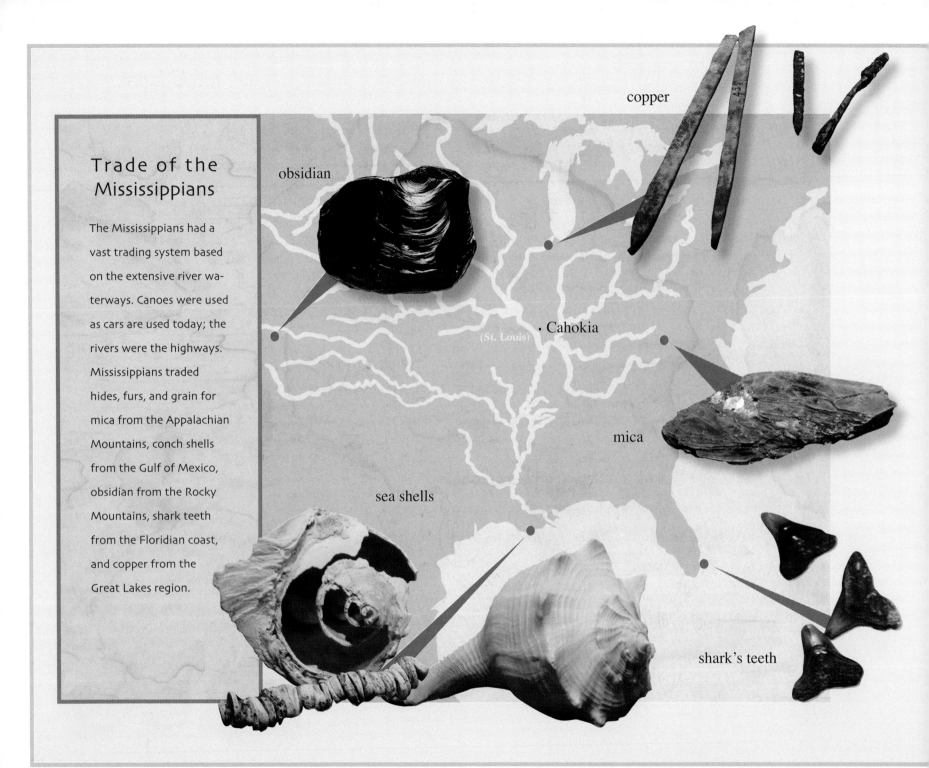

Trade of the Mississippians

The Mississippians had a vast trading system based on the extensive river waterways. Canoes were used as cars are used today; the rivers were the highways. Mississippians traded hides, furs, and grain for mica from the Appalachian Mountains, conch shells from the Gulf of Mexico, obsidian from the Rocky Mountains, shark teeth from the Floridian coast, and copper from the Great Lakes region.

copper

obsidian

(St. Louis)

• Cahokia

mica

sea shells

shark's teeth

ally added more earth to different mounds to build even bigger ones. This heavy labor was accomplished without the use of wheels or horses, because these things were unknown in this culture.

THE SOCIAL SYSTEM

The children of Cahokia were born into a highly organized society. People depended on each other and the roles they played in their society for their survival. This social system organized the people into four classes of society: the chief, the elite, the leaders, and the commoners. Some believe that slavery may also have been part of the social system.

The religious and governmental chief was called the "Great Sun." He was believed to be the brother of the sun. In this system, called "theocratic chieftainship," the chief claimed divine power as given to him by God. He and his family lived on top of the great platform mound now called "Monks Mound."

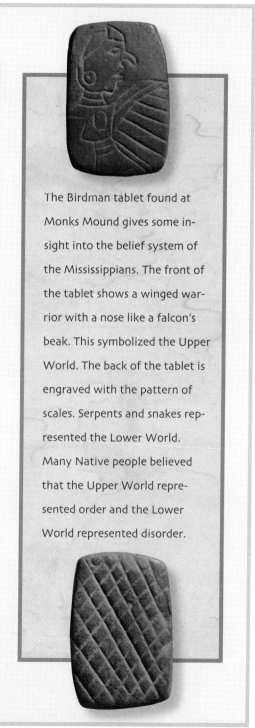

The Birdman tablet found at Monks Mound gives some insight into the belief system of the Mississippians. The front of the tablet shows a winged warrior with a nose like a falcon's beak. This symbolized the Upper World. The back of the tablet is engraved with the pattern of scales. Serpents and snakes represented the Lower World. Many Native people believed that the Upper World represented order and the Lower World represented disorder.

American Woodhenge

A circular sunrise calendar consisted of 48 large cedar posts arranged in a 410-foot diameter circled around a central observation post. It was probably used to determine the changing season, important to an agricultural way of life.

The elite class was made up of the Great Sun's relatives, priests, and lesser chiefs, who gave advice to the Great Sun. They were **privileged** people who did no labor and who also lived on top of Monks Mound.

The leaders were the heads of **clans** and communities. They were not born of noble birth, but were trusted by the elite class and **revered** by the commoners. The leaders designed and directed the construction of public buildings and supervised farming. They lived within the great **stockade** of the city. (This stockade was a fence made of 20,000 wooden posts, 20 feet high.)

COMMONERS

Most people were commoners who lived outside the stockade walls. The men of common status built and repaired the mounds and stockade fences. They hunted, fished, cut down timber, cleared the fields, and built the frames of the houses by lashing together tall poles. Some commoners were craftsmen, creating ceremonial artwork, tools, and weapons. Others were tradesmen or warriors who fought in battles and protected the city.

The women of common status cultivated the crops, gathered wild fruits and nuts, prepared all meals, cared for the children, and managed the home. They made pottery **vessels**, wove mats and baskets, and created cooking utensils of clay, wood, or shells. It was their job to

A Single Family House

prepare skins, sew clothing, and complete the building of their homes. To the tops and sides of the wooden frames, they added **thatched** roofs and attached skins and woven mats to create the walls.

People lived with their close relatives and extended families. Clans, or groups of these related families, lived in neighborhoods in different parts of the city, depending on their status. Single-family homes were built in rows around a large **plaza.** Houses of Cahokia's leaders stood safely inside the two-mile long stockade, which enclosed and protected the center of the city. Other houses owned by commoners were built outside the stockade, closer to the main farmlands.

AGRICULTURE AND POTTERY

For the first time in the history of the Mississippi Valley, the people grew as much food as they needed. The women grew corn, beans, squash, pumpkins, sunflowers and **gourds.** The corn, originally brought from Mexico, was the most important crop grown at Cahokia. It was the primary food in the Mississippians' diet. Surplus corn was stored in **granaries,** safe from rodents and the weather, to be distributed in times of **famine.** The Mississippians supplemented the crops they farmed with food from hunting, fishing, and gathering wild plants.

Two inventions made it possible to accumulate food in large quantities: the flint hoe and pottery. The flint hoe made it easy to break up the soil and weed between rows of corn. The Mississippians were among the first known of the early Americans to use their clay

Pottery

The clay figurine (found at Cahokia) represents a gardener cultivating the earth, shown as a cat-faced serpent. The serpent's tail has split into two squash vines that climb up her back — a symbol of agricultural fertility.

Flint hoe

pottery to store water and food. Pottery also was used to stew food, a method of cooking in which meat and vegetables were covered by water and slowly cooked over fire for many hours.

With abundant food, the population grew rapidly. Farming and permanent settlements allowed people time to develop skills for reasons other than survival (as compared to the nomadic hunters and gatherers, who constantly had to travel in search of food). The areas of arts, crafts, sports, and recreation flourished. The people made pottery in many shapes, including animals and humans. They designed jewelry from shells, beads, and copper.

THE POWER OF CORN

Those who controlled the corn controlled the other members of the community. The commoners were required to give much of the corn they grew as tribute to the clan leaders. Tribute was the act of showing appreciation or admiration. The clan leaders, in turn, gave the majority of the corn in tribute to the elite class, and to the Great Sun and his family. The upper class used the large amount of corn

Feeding the population of Cahokia required enormous amounts of corn on a daily basis. A typical meal would consist of corn prepared in different ways and a portion of stew made from nuts, pumpkin, and squash. On rare occasion, the villagers ate small amounts of meat.

to trade for household goods, jewelry, crafts, and other valuable items. These precious possessions, plus the control of the corn, made the Sun God and the elite class powerful and wealthy in the eyes of the common people.

It was rare, but on occasion, a commoner could improve his status. This might be accomplished through marriage, heroic deeds in war, or by payment of tribute in the form of valuable gifts to leaders.

THE MOUND BUILDERS DISAPPEAR

After 400 years of this type of city life, the population began to decline. Eventually all the people disappeared around 1400 C.E. What happened? Did they abandon Cahokia for some reason? Did they die from diseases? Did so many people in one area use up all the natural resources, such as timber and fertile soil? Some archeologists believe that the Mississippians suffered from a combination of severe drought and malnutrition from a diet based on too much corn and too little meat. To this day, their disappearance remains a mystery.

Explore the Cahokia Mounds State Historic Site in Collinsville, Illinois, just 10 minutes from downtown St. Louis. See the award-winning multimedia presentation and a replica of a village inside the museum. Walk by the Woodhenge calendar. Climb to the top of the 100-foot-tall, 14-acre Monks Mound, the largest prehistoric earthen construction north of Mexico. See if you can spot the other 68 mounds in the site.

HARVESTING LOTUS ROOT

CHAPTER THREE

THE OSAGE NATION

LATER NATIVE AMERICANS

Imagine, as a girl of 10 summers, you and your mother join the women of your extended family to dig the sacred roots of the water lotus in a nearby pond. Your younger sister plays with her doll as she watches Grandmother spread the lotus roots to dry. Your baby brother sleeps nearby in his cradleboard. You realize that, within three years, you will marry and have children of your own. You are a daughter of the great Osage Nation.

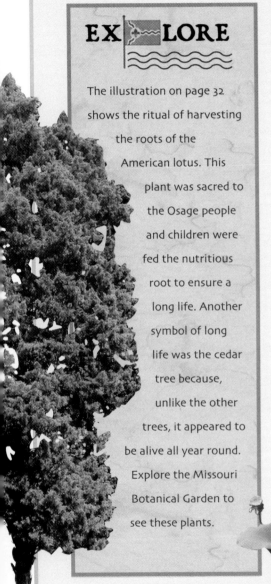

EXPLORE

The illustration on page 32 shows the ritual of harvesting the roots of the American lotus. This plant was sacred to the Osage people and children were fed the nutritious root to ensure a long life. Another symbol of long life was the cedar tree because, unlike the other trees, it appeared to be alive all year round. Explore the Missouri Botanical Garden to see these plants.

Cedar tree

American lotus

Our story continues near the Missouri River. Over the centuries, the mild climate, fertile land, great riverways, and abundant wildlife attracted other groups of native people to the land now called "Missouri." The Missouri and the Osage tribes were well established in the area when Europeans first traveled the Mississippi. The greater number of Missouri people lived north of the Missouri River. The Osage lived south of the Missouri River, as well as in parts of today's Arkansas, Kansas, and Oklahoma.

The Osage, who continue to live as a nation today in Oklahoma, migrated from the Ohio River Valley and shared religious symbols similar in spirit to the Mississippians. They called themselves WAH-SHA-SHE, "Children of the Middle Waters." Later, the French would change their name to "Osage." They were one of the most powerful tribes in the area, and their villages were scattered along the Missouri and Osage rivers. The principal village was built near the Osage River, a **tributary** of the Missouri River.

The Osage people were tall and strong, with broad shoulders. Most men were at least six feet tall, some seven feet tall. The men wore **loincloths**, **leggings**, and moccasins made of deer- or bearskins. In the winter they added deerskin shirts and buffalo robes. The men disliked facial hair and shaved their eyebrows and most of their heads, leaving a strip down the middle about three inches wide and two inches high.

Osage women wore simple dresses, leggings, and moccasins made of deerskin. Their long hair, parted in the middle, flowed loosely down their backs. The women dyed porcupine quills and sewed them in patterns on the clothes and moccasins worn for religious ceremonies. Both women and men wore bracelets, earrings, and tattoos.

SPIRITUAL BELIEFS

The Osage, as well as most native people of the Americas, had (and still have) a deep respect for nature. They lived in harmony with nature. The Osage worshipped an all-powerful sacred force called Wakontah. They believed Wakontah was the Creator that existed in all things, everywhere. Therefore, the Osage had a spiritual relationship to all things, living and nonliving, visible or invisible. The Osage called the sun "Grandfather," the moon "Grandmother," the earth "Sacred One." Because all things on which they depended, such as water, rocks, animals, and plants, came from the blessings of the sacred earth, the Osage believed that they needed to be caretakers of the earth and the life around them.

The sun was celebrated as the giver of life. Each day the whole village arose before sunrise. Women painted a red line in the part in

The red-tailed hawk - symbol of the warrior

Osage Warriors

Spider

The Osage believed that animals and plants had special powers and could lend their powers to people. Sub-clans chose a sacred animal: the hawk, black bear, buffalo, woodpecker, or spider, to be its symbol for life. The symbols represented such qualities as beauty, courage, strength, and quickness.

Here's how the spider was chosen:

When walking through the woods an Osage who was seeking a life symbol walked into a spider web. "Why don't you choose me as your symbol?" asked the spider. "What would make you a good life symbol for the great Osage?" asked the man with a laugh. And the spider answered, "Where I am, I build my house, and where I build my house, all things come to it."

their hair to symbolize the sun's journey across the sky throughout the day. As the sun rose, the people of the village went outside, placed moist soil on their foreheads, and greeted the sun with prayers of thanks. This **ritual** was repeated at midday and at sunset.

The simple daily tasks of the Osage, such as planting and hunting, had spiritual importance. Before beginning these tasks, they sent prayers through the thunder, the waters, the rocks, and the winds for good fortune.

The Osage believed that their world was made of relationships between opposite forces: dark and light, male and female, good and evil, visible and invisible, and creation and destruction. Following this belief system, the Osage divided the universe into two parts, the earth and the sky. They divided their population into two major clans, or groups of people related by blood. The clans were named "Sky People Clan" and "Earth People Clan." The two main clans were further divided into 24 sub-clans, with each clan choosing a life symbol. The people would call upon these sacred animal or plant life symbols before planting, hunting, or going to war.

ORGANIZATION OF SOCIETY

A chief and several priests were the leaders of each clan. Men held these positions of authority. The position of chief was **hereditary**, with the title and responsibility of the chief usually passed from father to son, who had to be worthy and qualified. When there was no son or if the son were considered unqualified, another male family member was chosen.

The chief's power was limited. His job was to see that his people were taken care of, including the elderly and less fortunate. He was not a ruler, but more of a leader of elected officials. The true governing body was a group of elderly men, the "Little Old Men." These elders were the keepers of the traditions and religious beliefs. They created religious ceremonies and explained the spiritual meaning of all aspects of life. The Little Old Men advised the chiefs, and the chiefs almost always followed their advice.

THE HOMES OF THE OSAGE

The Osage lived in villages on high hills or prairies that overlooked lower ground. They built their villages in locations near rivers, in

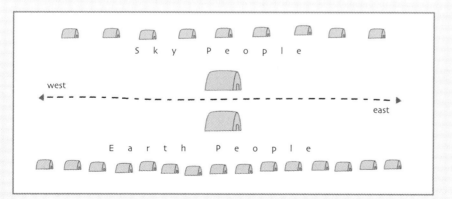

S k y   P e o p l e

west

east

E a r t h   P e o p l e

areas easy to defend. An Osage village was organized on a path running from east to west. The Sky People Clan, divided into 9 sub-clans, lived in homes

Roach

Clermont, a chief of the Osage Nation, was portrayed wearing a traditional Osage headdress called a "roach." The headdress was attached by braiding a lock of hair and a piece of hide connected to the headdress together, then securing both with a small bone or stick used like a hat pin.

Osage homes were built with multiple center posts that were notched to support a ridge pole. Over the ridge pole, smaller poles were bent to form the pitched roof. Wall posts completed the frame. The frame was covered in overlapping woven mats made of bark, skins, and long-stemmed marsh grasses called "rushes." Along the central pathway were one or more fireplaces used for cooking and heat. A smoke hole positioned in the roof above the fireplace let out smoke and allowed some light; still, the house remained somewhat dark and smoky. Circular storage pits were dug into the floor near a wall, and rectangular-shaped pits were used for trash.

constructed on the north side of the path, and the Earth People Clan, divided into 15 sub-clans, lived in homes on the south side. The village chiefs, one from each clan, lived in the center of the village, in houses built directly across from each other.

Large rectangular buildings about 20 feet wide and 40 feet long, called "longhouses," served as home for several families of a clan. Inside their homes were items that the Osage used each day. Woven mats covered the floor for sitting and sleeping. Pottery was used for cooking and storage. Gourds served as water containers. Each person possessed a wooden bowl. The Osage served food with spoons made of shell and horns. They used knives and their fingers, however, to eat the food. From the rafters and center post hung many things: dried meat stored in bags made of animal skin, strings of lotus root, dried pumpkin strips, and prepared **persimmon** cakes. The Osage also used rafters or walls to hang their clothes or their bow and quiver of arrows. They made all the objects found in the home from materials in the natural environment.

FAMILY AND COMMUNITY LIFE

The family and the clan arranged marriages among the Osage. A marriage was made between a member of the Sky Clan and a member of the Earth Clan. Girls often married at age 12, while boys usually married in their late teens or early twenties. An Osage man could marry more than one wife. His second wife was usually his first wife's younger sister, especially if the sister's husband was deceased. This arrangement provided the sister and her family with food, protection, and an inheritance. The new husband joined his wife's family.

Children were highly valued in Osage society because they were the future of the Osage Nation. Name-giving ceremonies were important events in the tribe. The clan priest chose a name for the child based on symbols of the father's clan and the sex and birth order of the child.

The first-born of each family held privileged positions. They were taught to be leaders of the community, and younger siblings were taught to follow their directions. The eldest daughter was given gifts and extra attention by her family and expected to do less work. The younger siblings were brought up to do the tribe's work. The children learned through example from the adults. They worked alongside their relatives, growing in skills and knowledge as they were given more challenging tasks. The extended family helped to raise and educate the children as if they were their own. Osage children called all their aunts "mother" and the men of their clan "uncle" or "grandfather."

When children disobeyed or showed unacceptable behavior, they were not physically punished. Instead, teasing

Cradleboard

The Osage considered Wakonta's most important blessing to be children. Babies spent their days wrapped in swaddling and secured to the cradleboard with a very wide belt. The boards, measuring three feet long and one foot wide, were carried or propped up. A projecting hoop guarded the infant's face in the event the board fell over, and attached bells entertained the child when brushed lightly. A cloth draped over the hoop protected the child from insects and sunburn.

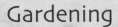

Gardening

In April, the beginning of the Osage New Year, women cleared the fields and planted rows of corn, pumpkin, squash, and beans. The crops were left unhoed and unfenced while the people left the village for the summer hunting expedition. When the Osage returned in the late summer, the crops were harvested and dried for the winter.

and shaming were used to get the younger children to obey. If stronger punishment was needed, they were ignored or ostracized, banished from the family home and activities. This method of punishment was very serious, as being together and sharing meals and communal activities were essential for happiness and survival.

RESPONSIBILITIES OF WOMEN

Although there were both medicine men and medicine women who healed the sick and wounded, and a few women became priests, males and females usually performed different jobs. Women and girls took care of the household and food preparation. They planted crops, prepared the meals, and preserved food for the winter. Women gathered wild berries, wild potatoes, prickly pear cactus, persimmons, milkweed sprouts, and nuts. Seeds such as sunflower seeds were roasted or eaten raw. The potato-like root of the lotus provided another important food source.

In addition to farming and food preparation, the women prepared skins, sewed clothing, made pottery, and cared for the younger children. Using only their fingers, they wove storage bags and belts for the cradleboard. They collected and dried rush grasses and wove rush mats to

Finger Weaving

cover the frames of houses. Girls practiced the skills of motherhood as they played with dolls and doll-sized cradleboards.

RESPONSIBILITIES OF THE MEN

In the Osage society, men had most of the power. They made the decisions of the family and the tribe. Men were responsible for providing the tribe with meat, for protecting the village, and for governing the people. Osage warriors protected their hunting territory and villages from other people who competed for the same resources. They protected the women and children, the future Osage generations, from any enemy who might threaten them. If an enemy was captured, it was the clan's chief who decided whether to spare the captive's life and adopt him into the tribe. War was regarded as necessary only for self-protection. It was one of the few situations where violence was acceptable. The tribe met for seven days before deciding to go to war, to give time to calm anger and consider consequences.

Boys learned skills from the men of their clan. They learned how to make and use bows and arrows. They learned to shape tools such as knives and flint scrapers. They played games
(continued on page 43)

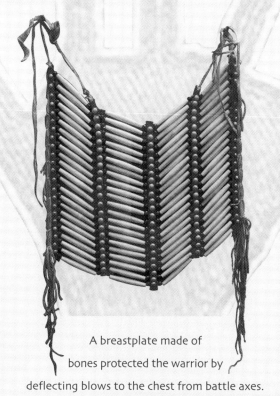

A breastplate made of bones protected the warrior by deflecting blows to the chest from battle axes.

Fire

Fire was held sacred as a piece of the sun. In fire, the forces of life and death were present. When controlled, it was the greatest of Wakonta's gifts. Fire warmed the cold, brought light into the dark, and made raw foods edible. Fire in a home symbolized the unity of the family. Uncontrolled fire, as in a prairie fire, was dangerous and destructive. When preparing for battle, warriors painted grotesque designs on their faces with charcoal. These designs symbolized the fierceness of the prairie fire and were meant to bluff and frighten their enemies. They also reminded the warrior that he fought to protect his family and the warmth of his home fire.

USES OF THE GREAT BUFFALO

The Osage used all parts of the buffalo. They ate the meat, including the most prized part, the tongue. They used the hide to make rope, shields, boats, drum heads, robes, carpets, and shelters. Bladders and intestines were used as bag-like containers for cooking or storing water. The Osage used the horns for eating or drinking utensils or placed them on headdresses of those of high honor in their tribe. They made glue and rattles from the hooves. Bones were used as needles and tools such as knives, shovels, and hoes. The women used the sinew as thread, and men used it as strings for their bows. Hair was used for paintbrushes and decorations. They used the tails for switches for swatting flies or to cool off while inside a sweat lodge. "Bison" is another name for this great animal of the plains.

Parfleche

WORKING WITH HIDE

Women prepared buffalo skins for use either by making them into stiff, hard rawhide or softening them for use as clothing. First, the fat, flesh, and fur were scraped off. Then the hide was washed and stretched on a frame. Rawhide, the uncured animal skin with its fur scraped off, was used to make storage bags called "parfleche." If the hide was to be softened, the woman would rub a mixture of animal brains and fat into the hide with a smooth stone. Men and women wore moccasins made from buffalo hides that still had the fur attached. In the winter, these moccasins could be turned with the fur to the inside, which kept their feet warm.

with toy bow and arrows to learn the necessary skills for hunting and becoming a warrior. As they grew older they began to help provide food for their families. Boys gathered birds' eggs and hunted pigeons, quail, rabbits, and squirrels with small bows. They learned to fish using nets, lines, and rock traps.

THE HUNT

Three times a year, the entire community, except for the very old and the very young, went on hunting **expeditions**. They went to western grasslands and prairies of today's western Missouri and Kansas. They hunted from May until August and then again from October to December for buffalo, elk, and deer. The fall hunt provided thick buffalo robes for the upcoming winter. In March, the Osage hunted in the forests for bear, beaver, and turkey. The clan chiefs organized the hunts and divided the meat among families. Along with their chosen warriors, the clan chiefs made sure the villagers were safe from enemy tribes while hunting and preparing the meat.

The Osage built dome-shaped **wigwams** as temporary homes during these trips, which the women maintained. The women butchered the animal, dried or smoked the meat, and prepared it for transport back to the village.

This was the lifestyle of the Osage for hundreds of years. However, their lives would change forever as newcomers arrived at their villages.

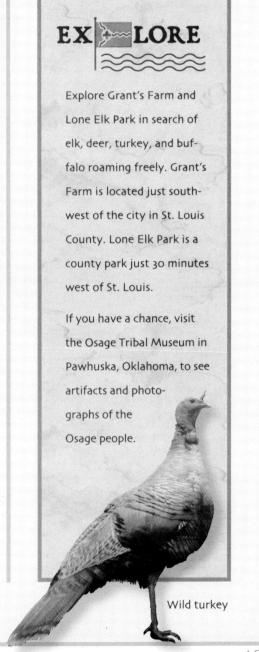

EX LORE

Explore Grant's Farm and Lone Elk Park in search of elk, deer, turkey, and buffalo roaming freely. Grant's Farm is located just southwest of the city in St. Louis County. Lone Elk Park is a county park just 30 minutes west of St. Louis.

If you have a chance, visit the Osage Tribal Museum in Pawhuska, Oklahoma, to see artifacts and photographs of the Osage people.

Wild turkey

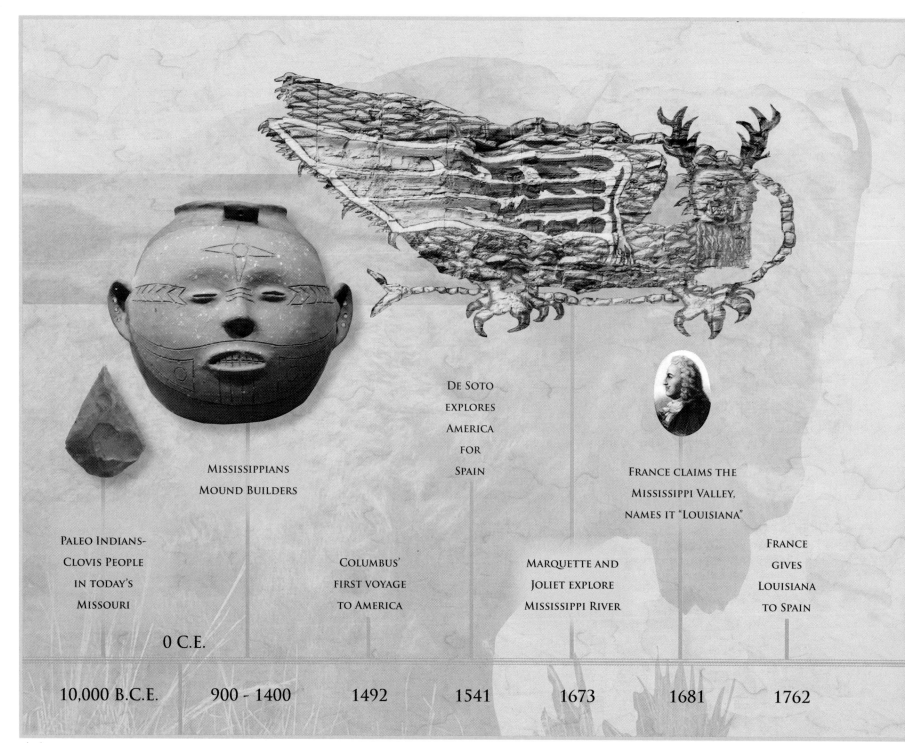

PALEO INDIANS-
CLOVIS PEOPLE
IN TODAY'S
MISSOURI

MISSISSIPPIANS
MOUND BUILDERS

COLUMBUS'
FIRST VOYAGE
TO AMERICA

DE SOTO
EXPLORES
AMERICA
FOR
SPAIN

MARQUETTE AND
JOLIET EXPLORE
MISSISSIPPI RIVER

FRANCE CLAIMS THE
MISSISSIPPI VALLEY,
NAMES IT "LOUISIANA"

FRANCE
GIVES
LOUISIANA
TO SPAIN

0 C.E.

| 10,000 B.C.E. | 900 - 1400 | 1492 | 1541 | 1673 | 1681 | 1762 |

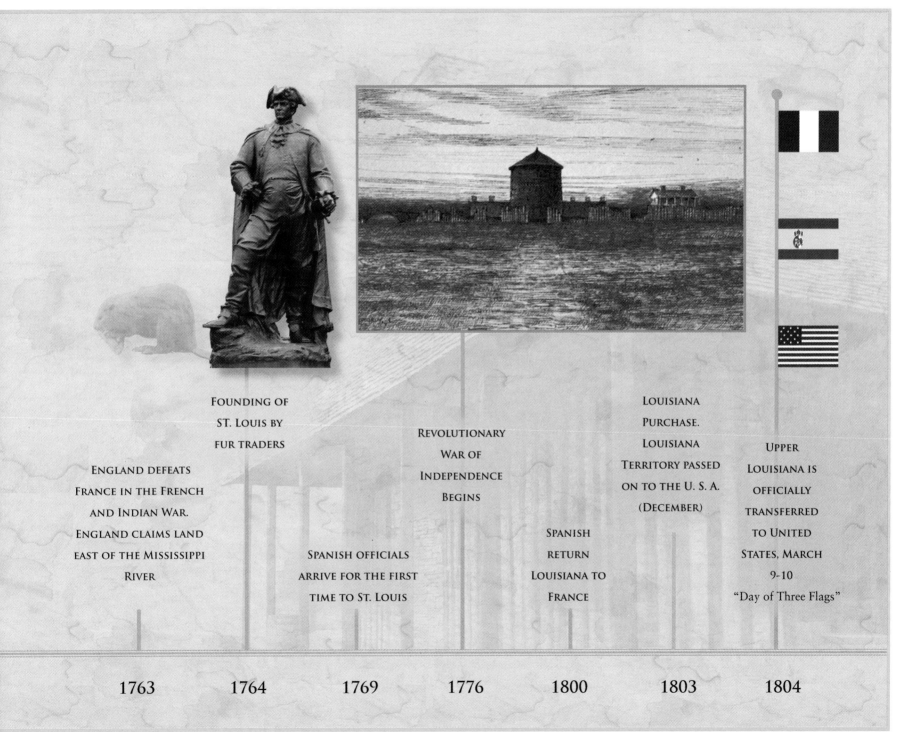

FOUNDING OF
ST. LOUIS BY
FUR TRADERS

REVOLUTIONARY
WAR OF
INDEPENDENCE
BEGINS

LOUISIANA
PURCHASE.
LOUISIANA
TERRITORY PASSED
ON TO THE U. S. A.
(DECEMBER)

ENGLAND DEFEATS
FRANCE IN THE FRENCH
AND INDIAN WAR.
ENGLAND CLAIMS LAND
EAST OF THE MISSISSIPPI
RIVER

SPANISH OFFICIALS
ARRIVE FOR THE FIRST
TIME TO ST. LOUIS

SPANISH
RETURN
LOUISIANA TO
FRANCE

UPPER
LOUISIANA IS
OFFICIALLY
TRANSFERRED
TO UNITED
STATES, MARCH
9-10
"Day of Three Flags"

| 1763 | 1764 | 1769 | 1776 | 1800 | 1803 | 1804 |

MARQUETTE AND JOLIET AT THE MEETING OF THE RIVERS

CHAPTER FOUR

EARLY EUROPEAN EXPLORERS

FROM COLUMBUS TO LA SALLE

Imagine you live in a crowded village in France about five hundred years ago. Your father wants to explore unknown territory across the Atlantic Ocean. He takes you and your family on a journey to this land, called the New World. When you arrive, you encounter people and animals that look strange to you. You travel through thickly forested lands on foot and paddle rivers in a boat made of tree bark invented by Native people, called a canoe.

Christopher Columbus

Columbus thought he had reached the Indies when he arrived at the chain of islands in the Caribbean. As a result, he called the people "Indians." Today the terms "Native American," "Native people," "American Indians," and "First People" are used as well as "Indians" to describe the indigenous or native population of the Americas. In Canada, "First Nation" is used. All are acceptable terms.

Our story continues in Europe long before the United States became a country. Europeans had a long tradition of travel and exploration, dating back to the **Crusades** and to the trade routes of **Marco Polo**. The desire of Europeans to spread Christianity, to accumulate wealth through trade, and to solve their overpopulation problems inspired them to travel beyond their national borders. Christopher Columbus was an Italian explorer who lived in the 15th century. He was a very well-educated man who read the stories of Marco Polo about the Far East, also called the "Indies" (now known as India and Southeast Asia). The stories described a land rich in minerals, exotic food, and spices.

In the 1400s, Europeans sailed south, around the tip of Africa, to get to the Far East. It was a long journey with dangerous waters, and they often encountered pirates. Travelers could go by land to the Indies, but they had to climb mountains, cross deserts, and cover land controlled by dangerous tribes. Those who made the difficult journey brought back exotic foods, spices, and cloth. Once the Europeans tasted exotic spices such as cinnamon, ginger, cloves, nutmeg, and pepper, they wanted more than just salt to flavor their food. (In those days food spoiled very easily with no refrigeration. Spices covered the smell and taste of rotting food.) They also desired rice, perfumes, fine silks, and precious stones from the East.

Columbus believed he could find a shortcut to the Indies by sailing west across the Atlantic Ocean. In 1492, he set out with his crew and his fleet of three ships, the *Niña*, the *Pinta*, and the *Santa Maria*. After a long and difficult journey, the

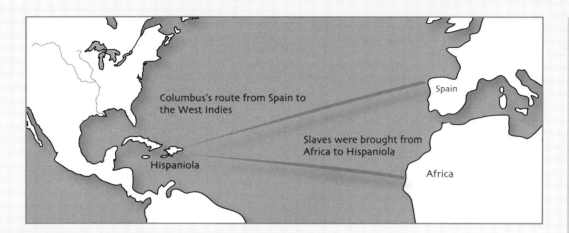

Columbus's route from Spain to the West Indies

Spain

Slaves were brought from Africa to Hispaniola

Hispaniola

Africa

ships reached a chain of islands. Columbus and his crew believed these islands were the Far East, the land they were seeking. They actually had arrived in a land that they did not know existed. Columbus called the people he met "Indians" because he believed they had arrived in the Indies. Spain later named the chain of islands the "West Indies." Eventually, Europeans came to call these islands and the massive continents nearby the "New World." By 1507, the continents would be called the "Americas," after the explorer Amerigo Vespucci.

SLAVERY IS INTRODUCED TO THE NEW WORLD

Columbus established the first Spanish **colony** in the New World on an island he named "Hispaniola." The Spanish who came later enslaved the Native people to mine for gold and work in the fields. When the Native people died because of exhaustion and European illnesses, slaves were brought to the West Indies from Africa.

Soon the Spanish realized that gold was plentiful in the region that is modern-

(continued on page 51)

America

Columbus may be credited with the European discovery the New World in 1492, but it was named after another explorer, Amerigo Vespucci. Vespucci explored parts of South America and claimed it to be a new continent. He published a book in 1503, called "Mundus Novus," or "New World." The stories of his travels were read all over Europe. In 1507, a German mapmaker decided to name the New World after Vespucci. He engraved a map on which he labeled the new lands "America" and the name stuck.

Explore the Black World History Museum located in North St. Louis. See a portion of a slave ship reconstructed to actual size. View the film clip that shows in greater detail how slaves were brought to this country in over-crowded boats. See devices used to control slaves, such as a whip and wooden leg shackles. Look for important information on contributions made to this area and the world by African Americans.

Slave handcuffs

A Brief History of Slavery

Slavery began in ancient times. In the first and second centuries, Egyptian, Roman, Greek, and Chinese armies enslaved people conquered in battles. Later Muslims, Italians, Spanish, and Portuguese developed an immense slave-trading system, purchasing people from African tribes to take to Europe as laborers. Slavery had long existed in Africa, where tribes captured and enslaved people of enemy tribes. European slave merchants bought their slaves from African rulers; later they became involved in capturing and selling slaves.

When the Spanish and the Portuguese, and later the English and French, began claiming ownership of the islands of the West Indies in the 15th to 16th centuries, they captured Native people to farm and work the gold mines. Most natives died from working in the mines or from European diseases. The conquerors then turned to Africa and brought slaves in by the thousands to work in the sugar cane fields, trading the slaves for guns, kettles, ammunition, and kegs of rum.

Captives were yoked together at the neck or linked together by chains to be transported from their homelands to the coast of Africa. Once onboard the ship, the captive people were chained together, lying side by side in the bottom of the boat. They were fed bread or rice for meals and taken to the top deck, where they were drenched with cold water for showers. The boat was purposefully overcrowded to make up for the many that would die en route from the terrible conditions or diseases. Slaves who died were cast overboard.

In the 1600s, England, France, and the Netherlands controlled the slave trade between Africa and the Americas. A Dutch ship brought slaves from Africa to Jamestown, Virginia, the first slaves brought to North America.

day Mexico. In 1519, Hernando Cortes led an army of 600 men into Mexico. Ships loaded with gold and silver returned to Spain. The mighty **Aztec** empire had been conquered. For the next hundred years, Spanish **conquistadors** overpowered Native people from Central America to South America in search of riches.

FIRST EUROPEANS IN THE ST. LOUIS AREA

In 1541, a Spanish explorer named Hernando De Soto was determined to find gold in the North American continent. He landed in today's Florida with 600 men. For six months, he and his men searched for gold in the Florida peninsula. Chopping their way through thick forests and swamps, they traveled into current-day Georgia, the Carolinas, Tennessee, Alabama, Oklahoma, and possibly Missouri. De Soto claimed all the land he explored for Spain.

As De Soto and his men pushed west in their search of riches, they killed many Native Americans. They took others as slaves. The Europeans unknowingly carried diseases for which the Native people had no **immunities**. Thousands of Native Americans died from **smallpox** and other European diseases. In 1541, the party crossed the Mississippi River into today's Texas. De Soto is credited as the first known European to discover the Mississippi River. By 1542, his men were exhausted, and De Soto died of fever. (An interesting tidbit of information: A city just south of St. Louis was named after De Soto.)

Another Spanish explorer, Francisco Vasquez de Coronado, traveled overland from Mexico, in the southwest of the continent, also in search of gold and riches.

El Adelantado Hernando de Soto.

Florida

Florida was discovered and claimed for Spain in 1512 by Ponce de Leon, who was in search of "the Fountain of Youth." He first saw land on Easter Day, and on account of the abundance and beauty of the flowers named the land "Pascua de Florida" (feast of flowers). Later, De Soto gave the name "Florida" to all the land he claimed for Spain.

It is unknown if he ever reached today's Missouri. No other known Europeans came to this area for more than 100 years.

FRENCH EXPLORERS SETTLE NEW FRANCE

Europeans still dreamed of reaching the Far East for its spices and silks. During the 1500s, the Spanish controlled the south Atlantic Ocean. Armed with cannons, their warships watched for any English or French ships. The English and French explorers steered their ships north to avoid the Spanish. They dreamed of finding an easy river route through the continent and called this imagined route "The Northwest Passage." In searching for the passage, Europeans explored North America.

In May 1497, an Englishman named John Cabot sailed north across the Atlantic Ocean and discovered what today is called Newfoundland. The French also looked for the Northwest Passage. In 1534, Jacques Cartier set sail and found the Gulf of St. Lawrence. That body of water led to the Great Lakes and to the interior of the continent. The French, by pure luck, had stumbled upon the only river system on the eastern coast that led into the interior of the continent. In the 16th century, the French claimed the St. Lawrence River and its **watershed** for their king. For approximately the next 200 years, the French were able to explore deep into the interior of the continent without competition from other European nations. In 1562, Quebec was founded, and, by the 1660s, the French had built a colo-

Algonquin

When the French settled in the Great Lakes region, they had moved to an area of the continent inhabited by Native Americans speaking dialects of the Algonquian language. The French coureurs-de-bois, who learned to speak Algonquin fluently, recorded many of the Algonquian names for the places they explored in the New World. The word Mississippi means "great river" in Algonquin.

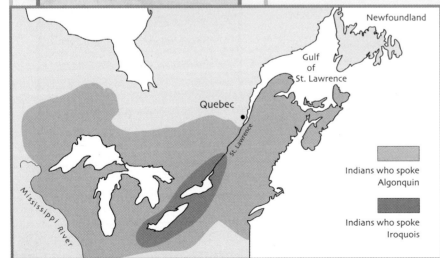

Newfoundland

Gulf of St. Lawrence

Quebec

St. Lawrence

Mississippi River

Indians who spoke Algonquin

Indians who spoke Iroquois

ny in North America called "New France." (An interesting tidbit of information: New France was later renamed "Canada." Canada means "village" in Iroquois.)

In 1607, English **colonists** settled at a site along the shores of Virginia that they named Jamestown after their king, James I. English colonists continued settling along the east coast of the continent. The Appalachian Mountains presented a natural barrier to the west, as did the dense forests that covered the eastern half of the continent. The English were slow to enter the middle portion of the continent. Taking possession of Indian land as they migrated westward, they based the building of their towns and farms on the traditions of the Old World.

MARQUETTE AND JOLIET

King Louis XVI of France dreamed of an **empire** and wanted to win control of North America. If a route could be found through the continent, it could help the French develop a rich source of trade with the lands of the Far East. Since the early 17th century, adventurers in the New World had heard of the mighty river that the Indians called the "Mesippi." The governor of New France ordered an expedition to discover if the Mississippi River flowed west into the Pacific Ocean, to see if it was the desired Northwest Passage.

Louis Jolliet was an experienced **voyageur-de-bois** (boatman) chosen to be in charge of the expedition. Jacques Marquette was a dedicated **Jesuit** missionary noted for his ability to speak the Algonquian language. In 1673, Marquette and Jolliet set out to discover whether this great river reached the Pacific Ocean. In his

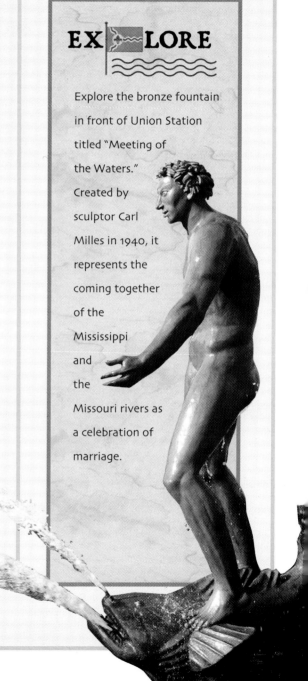

EX▶LORE

Explore the bronze fountain in front of Union Station titled "Meeting of the Waters." Created by sculptor Carl Milles in 1940, it represents the coming together of the Mississippi and the Missouri rivers as a celebration of marriage.

Explore the Confluence Greenway, a network of natural areas, outdoor recreational opportunities, educational facilities, and historical sites. See the confluence of the great Mississippi and Missouri rivers at Jones-Confluence Point State Park just 20 minutes north of downtown St. Louis. Take a walk or ride your bike across the mile-long Chain of Rocks Bridge (closed to motorized traffic), which crosses over Chouteau Island. Bike trails connect downtown St. Louis to many of these sites.

journal, Marquette noted the herd of 400 bison he saw on the shores, the great fish (possibly catfish) threatening to rip up their canoes, and a huge painting of two monsters on the bluffs along the eastern side of the river. But their greatest discovery came when they arrived at the **confluence** of the Missouri and Mississippi rivers (illustrated on page 46).

Paddling down the westward side of the Mississippi River, they saw a great disturbance in the water ahead. These are the words Marquette used to describe the event: "Sailing quietly in clear and calm water, we heard the noise of a rapid, into which we were about to run. I have seen nothing more dreadful. An accumulation of large and entire trees, branches, and floating islands, were issuing from the mouth of the river, with such **impetuosity** that we could not without great danger risk passing through it. So great was the agitation that the water was very muddy, and could not become clear." Marquette and Joliet are credited as the first Europeans to discover the Missouri River.

The expedition followed the Mississippi south to the Arkansas River. Friendly Indians told of hostile Spaniards living downriver. If the Frenchmen were captured or killed, the information they had gathered would not get back to New France and to King Louis. Also, they believed they had already learned what they had journeyed to find. The Mississippi River flowed south into the Gulf of Mexico, not westward into the Pacific. It was not the fabled Northwest Passage. After two months on the river, Joliet and Marquette decided to turn back to New France.

(continued on page 56)

How Missouri Got Its Name

When the Europeans came to North America, they entered a land of 500 nations. These nations were roughly organized into 10 language groups throughout the continent. Some of these languages were Algonquin, Iroquois, Souian, and Cherokee. Native speakers of Algonquian dialects extended from present-day Missouri to Maine along the Mississippi and St. Lawrence rivers. Tribes within a language group were friendly to each other, and the French became friends of Algonquin-speaking Indians living along the Great Lakes. Father Jacques Marquette moved to New France to convert Native people to Christianity and became fluent in Algonquin.

The Algonquins crafted beautiful, feather-light, birch-bark canoes that were easy to portage over the rough terrain between the rivers of the northeast. When the French arrived in the early 17th century, they quickly adapted Native canoes to their own use. In 1673, Marquette and Joliet traveled down the Mississippi in two birch-bark canoes. When the men came to the confluence, however, the rough waters threatened to rip apart their fragile boats. The Illinois, who spoke Algonquin, described the people who lived along this unruly river as great hunters and boatmen. These people rode the rough and rapid waters in canoes made of hollowed-out logs. The Illinois called these people "Missouri," a word in Algonquin meaning "people of wooden canoes." The French put the word "Missouri" on their maps to mark the place where the Missouri people lived. Over time it became the name of the river, the territory, and later the state.

dugout canoe

birch-bark canoe

EX LORE

Père Marquette State Park, an hour north from St. Louis, is named in honor of the priest Jacques Marquette. You will enjoy this beautiful scenic park, which overlooks the Illinois River. To get to the park, take the gorgeous Great River Road, which follows the Mississippi River. Look for the great Piasa Bird, originally painted on the bluffs by the Illini tribe, located at the Piasa Park in Alton, Illinois.

La Salle Claims Louisiana For France

Another Frenchman, named Robert Cavelier, Sieur de La Salle, paddled down the Mississippi River in 1682. At the mouth of the Mississippi River near present-day New Orleans, he claimed nearly half of the North American continent, including the huge watershed of the Mississippi, for the King of France. La Salle named the land "Louisiana" in honor of King Louis. Forts were soon built along the river to protect France's claim to the land and to promote fur trading west of the Mississippi.

This land had treasures that the Frenchmen wanted. Because French fashion included fur in its designs, most of the fur-bearing animals in Europe had been hunted to the point of extinction. Beaver fur was especially prized by the Europeans, and men could become wealthy in the New World by trapping the animal and selling the pelt to fashion-conscious Europeans.

French trappers and traders, called coureurs-de-bois, followed La Salle to the Missouri region. The typical coureur-de-bois was a young Frenchman who had left his homeland to seek freedom and adventure in the New World. He moved around the vast territory of Louisiana fearlessly, alone, and on foot. He stayed on

Robert Cavelier,
Sieur de La Salle

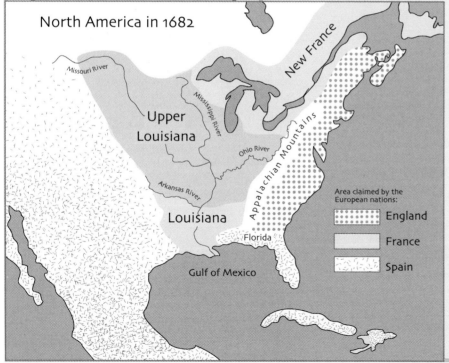

North America in 1682

Missouri River

New France

Upper Louisiana

Mississippi River

Ohio River

Appalachian Mountains

Arkansas River

Louisiana

Florida

Gulf of Mexico

Area claimed by the European nations:

England

France

Spain

Three European nations, France, England, and Spain, competed to control all of North America in the 1700s.

good terms with the Indians by adapting to their pattern of hunting and trading, learning their ways of survival in the wilderness, and by treating them with the respect accorded to equals. Adopting the practical fashion of leggings and moccasins from the Native American, the men wore hunting shirts made of tanned deerskin or coarse linen that hung to the knees and were belted and fringed. In the winter they wrapped themselves, Indian-style, in buffalo hide, or wore capotes (a hooded cape) in the French style. A cap made of fox, bear, or squirrel fur with ear flaps completed their winter wear. These men lived with the Indians, traded with them, spoke their language fluently, and sometimes took Indian wives.

The voyageur-de-bois (boatmen) used the waterways as the main transportation system. Though often difficult, the river was a preferred route to the overland paths through the wilderness. On foot, a trapper pushed through dense forests and underbrush and could carry only 50 pounds of goods on his back. When he reached the river, he could load his canoe with up to 150 pounds of goods and make about 12 to 15 miles a day paddling upstream.

LEAD IS DISCOVERED

In 1712, Antoine de La Mothe Cadillac was sent to Louisiana to search for silver. Instead, valuable lead and salt deposits were uncovered in what is now Madison County, Missouri. Lead was used for ammunition, and salt was important for preserving meat and fish. (An interesting tidbit of information: Cadillac went on to found the city of Detroit, the largest car-manufacturing city in the United States.

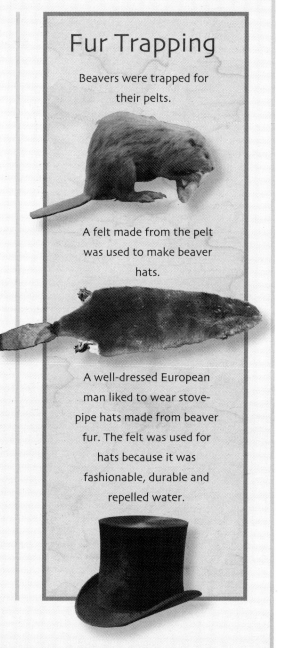

Fur Trapping

Beavers were trapped for their pelts.

A felt made from the pelt was used to make beaver hats.

A well-dressed European man liked to wear stove-pipe hats made from beaver fur. The felt was used for hats because it was fashionable, durable and repelled water.

The Cadillac car was named after him.)

In 1718, New Orleans was founded on the eastern bank of the Mississippi near the Gulf of Mexico, and in 1722 the city became the capital of the Louisiana Territory. In 1720, Fort de Chartres, the capital of **Upper Louisiana** was built on the east bank of the Mississippi, in the Illinois territory. West of the Mississippi, Philippe Renault, an ambitious mining promoter, set up the first extensive lead mines in 1720. He brought 200 workers, including slaves from the West Indies, to the area and imported mining tools manufactured in France. His main mining operations were on the **Meramec** River and in the area around Mine La Motte. He continued this operation for about twenty years. With the discovery of the lead mines on the western side of the river, many French settlers moved from Illinois territory to current-day Madison County, Missouri. Ste. Genevieve was founded in 1735 (the first permanent settlement in present-day Missouri) on the west bank of the Mississippi, and a road was built from that settlement to the nearest lead mines.

FRENCH AND AFRICANS SETTLE THE AREA

French explorers appeared in the region with increasing frequency. Following the earliest explorers, people of New France came into Illinois territory to establish **missions**, trading posts, and mining operations. The first two settlements in the area were on the east side of the Mississippi at Cahokia (1699) and Kaskaskia

(1700). French families began to settle on the eastern banks of the Mississippi, near the French fort, Fort de Chartres. Soon afterward French **missionaries** founded the village of Cahokia, across the river just southeast of present-day St. Louis. Priests brought slaves to the missionary. (An interesting tidbit of information: This Cahokia, which continues today as a modern suburb east of St. Louis, is located southwest of the ancient "Mound City" of Cahokia. "Cahokia" was the name of a tribe of Native people living in Illinois territory long after the Mound Builders when the French began to settle in the area. However, their namesake is given to both of these communities.)

This was the beginning of French and African settlers moving to live in the area we know as present-day Missouri. They joined the Missouri and Osage, who were already living in the region, as well as the Fox, Sauk, Delaware, Cherokee, Miami, Shawnee, and Kickapoo, among other tribes. Many of these tribes were forced to move from the eastern woodlands to west of the Mississippi River as a result of the ever-growing English settlements.

Indian Influences

American Indians introduced Europeans to canoes, moccasins, leggings and other deerskin clothing, methods of farming, corn, popcorn, potatoes, the sweet potato, pumpkins, tomatoes, and tobacco. (An interesting tidbit of information: The Iroquois nation demonstrated a form of self-government that inspired our forefathers when creating the Constitution. The Iroquois believed that all people were equal and had a voice in their government. This was different from European monarchies, where one ruler made all the laws for his subjects.)

FEBRUARY 15, 1764

CHAPTER FIVE

FRENCH SETTLERS

THE FOUNDING OF ST. LOUIS

Imagine you are a 14-year-old boy charged with the building of a settlement ... in the middle of the wilderness ... in the winter of 1764. Your stepfather has left you in charge of a crew of 30 men, made up of hired hands and slaves. You and the men must clear the land and begin the construction of a fur-trading post, which one day will develop into a fine French village.

Pierre Laclède

Pierre Laclède was the second son of a prominent family from southern France. As was the custom of the times, only first-born sons inherited the land or property of their father. Laclède could have sought a career in the church or military if he remained living in France. Instead he came to the New World, as did many European second-born sons, to seek his fortune.

This part of our story begins in 1762, with a man named Pierre Laclède. Laclède was a well-educated Frenchman who had come to New Orleans in 1757. He had a partner named Antoine Maxtent who was a wealthy merchant. Their company obtained a trading agreement from the French governor of Louisiana to trade with the Indians of the Mississippi and Missouri rivers. This area was called Upper Louisiana and was located in the northern section of the Louisiana Territory, which contained today's Missouri. The agreement gave the Maxtent, Laclède and Company a trade **monopoly**, which meant that they were the only French company allowed to trade for furs with the tribes. In exchange for the furs, the Native Americans received items such as cloth, blankets, shirts, guns, powder, flints, knives, beaver traps, kettles, hatchets, and hooks. In their agreement, Maxtent would provide the money to buy the trade goods. Laclède would travel to Upper Louisiana to establish a trading post and to manage the fur trade on the Missouri River. Laclède was an **ambitious** man who believed that fur trading in America would bring him wealth.

Shortly after the fur-trading agreement was signed, however, Laclède received troubling news. All the land east of the Mississippi River once claimed by France was now under English control.

THE FRENCH AND INDIAN WAR

As the **British** colonies became more populated, the colonists looked west of the Appalachian Mountains for new land to settle. The French, who claimed the entire watersheds of the Mississippi and St. Lawrence rivers, which included the Great

Lakes and the Ohio River Valley, wanted the Ohio River Valley to remain under French control. The conflict began in 1754, when George Washington, leading a unit of Virginia soldiers, ambushed a French scouting party at Fort Duquesne (near present-day Pittsburgh). The war that followed was called the French and Indian War because Native Americans joined in battle on both sides. Those that joined the French side were afraid that the British would take away their land. The fighting ended and the French were defeated in 1759. With the signing of the Treaty of Paris on February 10, 1763, France surrendered all of its North American territory east of the Mississippi, with the exception of New Orleans, to England.

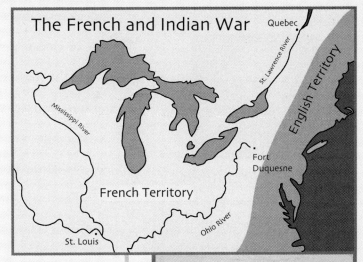

The French and Indian War

AN IDEAL SITE

Laclède wanted to establish more than just a trading post in Upper Louisiana. His dream was to build a fine French village where he could raise his children. He wanted to bring other educated French people to the village. In late summer of 1763, Pierre Laclède and his stepson, Auguste Chouteau, age 13, started out from New Orleans with 20 boatmen and began to travel up the Mississippi. The boatmen paddled, towed or poled the pirogues (flat-bottomed boats) against the river's current, traveling about 10 miles a day. The boats were loaded with merchandise from France to trade with the Native American tribes living near the Missouri River. After three months of traveling, the men arrived at Fort de Chartres and

Numbers of Settlers

The French empire covered almost half of the North American continent at the beginning of the war. The territory was occupied by about 80,000 French settlers. In contrast, the 13 British colonies were settled by almost 2 million people living along the eastern seaboard. France hadn't settled a large enough population to defend the vast French empire containing New France and Louisiana.

Madame Chouteau

Auguste's mother originally lived in New Orleans. After giving birth to Auguste, she left her husband because of his cruelty. Years later, Madame Chouteau moved to St. Louis, accompanied by Laclède. She lived in a house he had built for her. She was the first European woman to live in St. Louis. Respected, admired, and loved by the French townspeople, Madame Chouteau was called "La mère de St. Louis." It is French for "the mother of St. Louis."

spent the winter on the east side of the Mississippi River, in Illinois Territory.

In December, Laclède and Chouteau left the fort to search for a good place to build the trading post. They found a **bluff** on the west bank of the Mississippi River about 15 miles downstream from the confluence of the Mississippi and Missouri rivers. (An interesting tidbit of information: Several earthen mounds constructed by the Mississippian mound-building culture surrounded the site.)

The high bluff made a great lookout for enemies and provided safety from flooding. The river would provide ample water, even if a little muddy, for the home. A nearby stream could be used in the future to provide the waterpower needed for **mills** to grind wheat into flour. There was an ample supply of timber and limestone to build homes and stockades. Prairie land west of the river would make good farmland and provide pasture for livestock. Laclède said to Chouteau, "I have found a site on which to form my settlement which might hereafter become one of the finest cities in America." (-from the journal of Chouteau.)

This site was ideal for the new settlement. Laclède slashed tree trunks to mark the spot, and the boy and man returned to Fort de Chartres. Two months later, in February of 1764, Laclède sent his stepson back to the site. Commanding a crew of 30 men, including slaves, Chouteau supervised the construction of the trading post (illustrated on page 60). Auguste Chouteau was barely 14 years old, but Laclède placed him in charge of this important project. In Chouteau's time, boys who displayed intelligence and responsibility were given positions of authority. Chouteau could read, write, and follow the written details of Laclède's plans. He directed the men to clear the land, build a warehouse for the company merchandise, and construct cabins for the workers. Laclède's dream of "one of the finest cities in America" began on February 15, 1764. Laclède named the trading post "St. Louis," in honor of King Louis IX, a kind and just French king who died in the Crusades and was made a saint in 1297.

FAMILIES MOVE TO ST. LOUIS

When Laclède established St. Louis early in 1764, he knew that French settlers living east of the Mississippi were unhappy with the transfer of Illinois territory to the British. They did not want to live under British laws or English religion. France was a Catholic nation; England was Protestant. Laclède invited these French-speaking people to his newly established settlement. Many families chose to move across the river to St. Louis instead of downriver to New Orleans. Over time, other French people moved to St. Louis from New Orleans, Canada, and France. Within a year of its founding, about 50 French families were settled in St. Louis. It was Laclède's good fortune to establish St. Louis at just the right time to attract many French people looking for a friendly place to relocate.

(continued on page 67)

St. Louis

King Louis IX of France
Born 25 April 1214
at Poissy, France
Died 25 Auguste 1270
at Tunis, Algeria
Canonized 1297

Saint Louis stands in history as the ideal king for the Middle Ages. He was a brave knight, a wise jurist, and a compassionate king. He felt he was responsible, before God, for the welfare of his people. He built hospitals and orphanages for the blind and lepers. He loved justice and established the first court of appeal.

UNEXPECTED VISITORS

One spring while the men were building the settlement of St. Louis, several hundred Missouri appeared. The first thought of the settlers was to grab their guns to protect themselves. They soon realized that women and children accompanied the men. This was a signal that the warriors did not come to fight and that no battle was expected.

Through sign language, the Missouri people expressed their desire to live in the new village. Missouri warriors had traveled from their village 180 miles away, bringing their wives, children, dogs, and horses. They were hungry and expected to be offered meals and gifts, as this is their custom when Native Americans received visitors.

Chouteau knew his men barely had enough supplies for themselves. He also knew that many French families feared Native Americans. They would not move to St. Louis if Natives lived among them. Chouteau sent for his stepfather.

While waiting for Laclède's return, Chouteau asked the Missouri people to help build the homes for the settlement. In the Native American culture, construction of homes was the job of women. While the Missouri men relaxed by the fires, the women and children dug the foundation of Laclède's house. The earth was carried away in large wooden platters or baskets balanced on their heads. Chouteau paid them in vermilion (red dye), verdigris (green dye), and awls. For 15 days, the Missouri people stayed on the site while the trading post was constructed. For 15 days, Chouteau waited for the return of his stepfather.

Upon his return, Laclède gave the Missouri leaders gifts of corn, cloth, guns, and ammunition. He told them they could have more of these items in exchange for furs. The Missouri chiefs told Laclède they were like ducks and geese that sought open water in order to rest. The settlement would be a safe and easy place for them to live. Laclède said that if they follow the example of ducks and geese, they followed bad guides. Eagles and other birds of prey would easily discover them if they lived near open water. Ducks and geese were safer under a bush or in the woods. Laclède told the Missouri that enemy warriors would attack and kill the men and make their women and children slaves, if they knew the Missouri chose to lived openly. Laclède convinced the Missouri that they were safer in their own village in the woods. He welcomed them to come back in smaller numbers to visit and trade.

Satisfied and impressed with Laclède's leadership, the Missouri returned to their villages. Friendly terms were maintained for many years between the French settlers of St. Louis and the Missouri people.

Building the Village

Laclède wanted to build a village patterned after those he knew in France. The French were a social people who enjoyed each other's company. The village would be designed as a community where residents share land and resources. The village plan had three distinct areas:

(1) "Residential" - divided into blocks and lots where the settlers built their houses, slave quarters, barns, chicken coops, stables, and tool sheds. It included areas for orchards and small kitchen gardens. (An interesting tidbit of information: the French combined homes, businesses, and farms throughout their village. Business was conducted in the homes or on the street. The English, in contrast, preferred to keep their businesses in a separate location known as a business district.)

(2) "Commons" - wooded land where the villagers could hunt and graze their pigs, cows, and horses, as well as gather firewood, nuts, and berries.

(3) "Common field" - a fertile area divided into long, narrow sections or strips. A strip was assigned to each family for growing crops. The settlers planted, cultivated, and harvested their crops of Indian corn, wheat, barley, oats, beans, pumpkins, flax, tobacco, and cotton. Their tools were simple: a hoe, **sickle**, spade, axe, rake, and pitchfork. Oxen pulled plows and farm carts.

In the residential area, Laclède laid out a **grid** of 49 blocks facing the riverfront. Each block was quartered into sections called "lots." To encourage settlement,

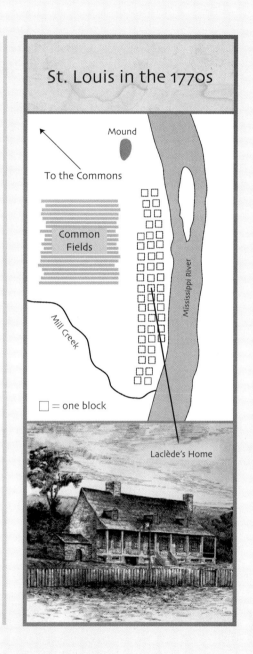

St. Louis in the 1770s

Mound

To the Commons

Common Fields

Mississippi River

Mill Creek

☐ = one block

Laclède's Home

EXPLORE

Explore Cahokia State
Historic Site and Holy
Family Church in Cahokia,
Illinois, to see traditional
colonial French architec-
ture. Visit the museum to
learn the history of early
French settlers. Cahokia is
the oldest French settle-
ment along the Mississippi
River (even older than
New Orleans!). It was settled in 1699. It's only 10
minutes from downtown
St. Louis.

Laclède assigned lots without charge to the first settlers of St. Louis. Although he had no legal right to do this, the proper authorities later recognized his grants. He

English construction

gave one lot to each family on which to build their houses. The lots measured about 120 feet wide by 150 feet long. To families who had more money or were of higher status, he assigned two or more lots. Stockades were built around each lot.

The French built houses in a different manner than the English. The English stacked long, squared-off logs, one on top of one another horizontally, to build the

French construction

walls of the cabin. The spaces and cracks between the logs were then filled with small strips of wood and a type of plaster made from a mixture of clay and straw.

The early settlers of St. Louis built homes in the French tradition. They positioned logs next to one another vertically, much like building a stockade. The spaces between the logs were filled with stones. A paste made of mud and moss or straw glued everything together. Doors were cut from thick wooden planks. The men cut simple windows through the walls. Shutters were positioned on each side of the window opening, and the hole was covered over in cold weather. (An interesting tidbit of information: As people moved to St. Louis from across the river or upriver from New Orleans, they brought doors and windows from their old houses to reuse in their new homes.)

Steeply pitched roofs were covered in shingles. The shingles were made from short logs split into strips. Because iron nails were rare, wooden pegs were used to hold the shingles in place. The edge of the roof extended far beyond the walls. This design allowed the roof to quickly shed rainwater and kept the plaster walls dry. A large porch, called a gallerie, was built around the house.

CAPTAIN DE BELLERIVE

Captain Louis St. Ange De Bellerive was the commandant at Fort de Chartres, the French Capital of Upper Louisiana. When all French territory east of the Mississippi (including the fort) was officially transferred to the English, De Bellerive and the residents of Fort de Chartres moved across the river to St. Louis. They included officers and soldiers who guarded the fort, craftsmen, and traders. St. Louis became the new capital of Upper Louisiana Territory; and De Bellerive, as the ranking French official in St. Louis, continued to represent the French government in Upper Louisiana.

Captain De Bellerive was known for being fair, respectful, and experienced in dealing with Native Americans. He set up in St. Louis the common law of the time in Paris:

- Males from the age of 14 could vote for town officials.
- Slaves were to be instructed and baptized in the Catholic religion.
- It was forbidden to use extreme punishment on slaves, including separating families by selling family members to different owners.

EXPLORE

Explore Bellerive Park, named in the Captain's honor, on the bluffs of the Mississippi River in Carondelet. This neighborhood was originally a small French village that was later added to the City of St. Louis. The park gives an excellent panoramic view of the river, woods, and sandbars. It is very much as the area may have been when Laclède and Chouteau first traveled the Mississippi in 1763.

See the statue of Pierre Laclède, erected in honor of his founding of St. Louis, on the west side of City Hall. The offices of the mayor of St. Louis and city lawmakers are located here.

Once Laclède was released from his governmental responsibilities, he devoted his time to developing the fur trade in St. Louis. Traders came to the growing settlement for goods from Laclède's warehouse. The traders paddled their canoes far up the Mississippi and Missouri rivers to exchange the European-made items for furs from local tribes. They returned, bringing the furs and skins to Laclède, who took the pelts and gave them newly delivered trade items from New Orleans. Laclède then pressed the furs into packs weighing between 80 and 100 pounds and sent the packs downriver to New Orleans for shipment to France. St. Louis quickly became the commercial and cultural center of Upper Louisiana because of the success of the fur trade. Only five years after the village was established, between 1,200 and 1,500 packs of furs had been **exported** to France.

By 1770, records show a population of 500 residents in St. Louis (about one of every three people was black). The village numbered 15 stone houses and 100 wooden cabins. Laclède purchased Maxtent's share of the business when the company lost its trade monopoly and Maxtent ended the partnership. This put Laclède deeply into debt. He left St. Louis in 1777 to meet with Maxtent in New Orleans to sort out his financial affairs. While on the return voyage to St. Louis on May 27, 1778, Pierre Laclède died suddenly. He was buried near the Arkansas River. Still, in the 14 years since he first traveled to Upper Louisiana and founded the trading post, Laclède had begun to realize his dream. St. Louis was becoming a fine French village.

LIFESTYLES OF THE PEOPLE

The Laclèdes and Chouteaus were families of wealth and education. Their large houses were built of limestone and furnished with fine furniture from France. In their homes, articles such as silverware, crystal glasses, books, and ornate four-poster beds were to be found. Some of the wealthy residents sent their children to France or Quebec for education.

Most French settlers lived humble lives. In their simple log homes one could find a bed, table, chairs, cupboard for kitchen supplies, trunk, and dresser. Fewer than one in 20 people of early St. Louis could read or write. For the first 10 years of St. Louis existence, there were no schools. The first school was established in 1774, and it was a private school for sons of leading families. A private school for girls was started in 1797. (An interesting tidbit of information: It would not be until 1833 that public schools were established in St. Louis.)

CLOTHING

For everyday wear, French settlers dressed in simple clothes. Women wore long **calico** skirts made of blue or red cotton cloth over several petticoats and a short cotton jacket. They sometimes wore an apron made of deerskin. In colder weather, a long cotton or heavy wool cape was added. Men and women often went barefoot in mild weather. When there was a need to wear shoes, the French wore moccasins. They wrapped their heads, turban style, with red or blue handkerchiefs.

Fancy Clothes

When it was time for parties and dances, the wealthier of the French settlers dressed in elegant fashion. Men tied back their hair with ribbons and powdered it white to mimic the style of France. They wore fancy coats and vests with trim of lace or gold buttons. Fancy shoes with silver buckles completed the formal wear. Many women wore fine silk or satin dresses, beautiful jewelry, and fancy combs in their hair. They sometimes carried ornately decorated fans in their hands.

Money

In the early days of the village, little currency was available, nor was it necessary. People grew, gathered, hunted, or fished for food. They bartered for goods or work that needed to be done. Because fur trading was the chief occupation for settlers in St. Louis, furs and deer hides (called peltry) were used as money. This is where the term "buck" for money originally came from; a buck is a male deer. When people bought a small amount of items, they received change in goods. Sometimes change was given in needles, pins, or a small packet of writing paper.

The men wore cotton **breeches** and shirts in summer. They grew their hair long and tied it back with large blue handkerchiefs. In cooler weather, the men wore pants and shirts made of buckskin. Hooded capes (called "capotes"), fur hats, stocking caps, and mittens were added protection from the cold in the winter. Men kept their knives, tobacco, flint for starting fires, and other important items they called their "necessaries" in pouches hung from their belts with leather straps.

Slaves wore simple shirts, pants, or dresses made of rough cloth. They were at the mercy of their owners for obtaining new clothes when the old ones were worn out or outgrown.

ROLES OF THE FRENCH MEN

Fur trading was the primary occupation, and most men who came to live in St. Louis were traders. They left St. Louis for months at a time, especially during the fall and winter, to trade with the Indians. This was the time when the animals grew their thick winter coats. Some coureurs-de-bois traveled westward and did their own trapping instead of trading.

When in St. Louis, these men were farmers, growing corn, wheat, potatoes, pumpkins, melons, cabbages, beets, and carrots in the common fields. They harvested grapes, apples, plums, and peaches from their garden orchards. They grew tobacco to smoke and **hemp** to make rope. The settlers of St. Louis raised cattle, horses, hogs, and chickens to provide meat, eggs, milk, butter, and cheese. (An interesting tidbit of information: The French ate horsemeat and still do.) To supplement their diets, almost all the men hunted. Deer, bear, rabbit, squirrel, raccoon, possum, turkey, ducks, pheasant, and quail were plentiful in the nearby forests. Fish, clams, and mussels were abundant in the rivers and streams.

ROLES OF THE FRENCH WOMEN

The women did much of the work to care for their families. They prepared food, kept the homes clean, washed and repaired clothing, and raised the children. They tended gardens, milked cows, collected eggs, and gathered nuts, berries, and seeds. Most meals were stews with lots of vegetables, a little deer or horse-meat, and bear fat cooked in a pot over a fire. (A stew called "jambalaya" was also popular. First created by slaves in New Orleans, it was a mixture of rice cooked with fish, sausage, and/or chicken, and spices.) Vegetables, fruit, nuts, and seeds were gathered, dried, and stored for winter. From a young age, children were expected to help with the many chores.

While the men were away hunting, trapping, and trading, the women took care of business. French women were seen as partners with their husbands. They had many rights not common for women at that time. Some owned their own property or businesses. (An interesting tidbit of information: Ownership of land or business was unheard of for English women. The only people who could own property and busi-nesses, as well as make legal decisions, were men. Not so in the French culture; the women were treated more as equals.)

Laundry

Cleaning clothes was back-breaking work. Clothes had to be soaked, boiled and beaten, and scrubbed on washboards. Then the laundry was rinsed and wrung out by hand, then dried in fresh air. Later the clothes would be pressed. Irons, made of a solid piece of cast iron and a cast iron han-dle, were heated in a fire. The handle would heat up along with the iron itself. Many women burned them-selves be-cause the handle was almost as hot as the bottom of the iron!

Slave Auctions

Most slaves bound for St. Louis were brought from Africa to the West Indies. From there they were taken to New Orleans and sold at auction. The slaves were washed, shaved, and rubbed with palm oil before the auction. This was done to disguise sores and wounds caused by confinement on the slave boat. The overseer placed the slave on the auction block, as if he were livestock. Buyers examined the African. They pulled open his mouth to see his teeth, pinched limbs to feel his strength, made him walk up and down to detect any signs of lameness, and made him stoop and bend in different ways to detect any concealed rupture or wound.

Slaves came to St. Louis with the first settlers to help build the settlement. Slave ownership was a mark of status among the French settlers. Typically, the French owned one or two slaves per family, four or five if they were wealthier. The slaves lived in separate buildings behind their owners' homes, or in cellars of smaller homes.

An entire way of life in early St. Louis depended on the labor of slaves. In general, slaves worked six days a week for ten to twelve hours a day — from 6 a.m. to noon with an hour break, and then 1 p.m. until dark. They labored hard for their owners. The men cleared land, planted and cultivated crops, hunted, rowed boats, and mined lead and salt. Many Africans had been skilled craft workers in their homelands and were put to work as carpenters, metalworkers, blacksmiths, or barrel makers.

Enslaved women cooked, did laundry, performed other household chores, and cared for their owners' children. They took on the duties of servants, nurses, dressmakers, and cooks, and worked in the fields. Chores for their own families awaited them at the end of the day, and their work continued at home before they could rest. In some cases, slaves did all the work for the owners' families. But in many cases, the French worked side by side with their slaves.

The French laws concerning slavery were called the Code Noir (Black Codes). Slaves were the property of their owner and, as property, had no rights. They could not own property or be legally married. However, the laws did allow slaves to hire themselves out as farmers, laborers, craftsmen, hunters, and trappers.

There were also enslaved Native people in St. Louis. Some tribes captured people of enemy tribes and traded them as slaves with the French for various goods. Many influential people, such as Laclède, Madame Chouteau, and Captain St. Ange De Bellerive had Native slaves.

FREE BLACKS

Not all blacks were enslaved. Some free blacks moved to St. Louis from other areas. Many were born of parents from different races. Others were set free by their masters or earned their freedom by working for pay in their free time.

Free blacks worked in many different jobs or businesses. They worked as domestic servants, at the riverfront on the docks, on boats going up and down the river, and in mills or warehouses. Some set up their own businesses as trappers, tanners, blacksmiths, gunsmiths, cabinetmakers, coopers, barbers, laundresses, and owners of bathhouses or boarding houses. Some free blacks in the later years of the village became teachers and ministers. Others became financially well off by inheriting and investing in real estate. Others leased property to newly arriving **immigrants** or developed large-scale butcher or hauling businesses. Over time, a middle and upper class of blacks and people of mixed racial background developed.

EXPLORE

Explore the Missouri History Museum in Forest Park to learn more about the fur trade. See real traps and a beaver pelt. Visit the exhibit on Jeanette Fourchet, a free black woman in early St. Louis. She was allowed to own property, including her house and a strip of land in the common field. Several tools and other pieces of furniture are on display. She probably worked as a cook and did the laundry for people in early St. Louis.

EX

LORE

Explore Soulard Market, a farmer's market since 1779. Julia Soulard, Auguste Chouteau's sister-in-law, donated the two-block area to the city with the understanding that it always be used as a public market.

(An interesting tidbit of information: Jacques Claymorgan was a man of mixed racial background who moved to St. Louis from the West Indies. Claymorgan was an early explorer of the West, searching for land routes to the Pacific Ocean long before the Lewis and Clark expedition. Claymorgan Alley on Laclède's Landing was named after him.)

Although free, St. Louis residents of African or mixed descent were not citizens. They could not vote, testify in court against a white person, or live in the city without a license. Some free blacks lived side by side with the French. People of all races and classes attended the only Catholic church together.

SUNDAYS

For most people, Sunday was a day to look forward to. The shared good times bonded the community. Festivities were held on Sundays and church holidays. After the church service, the family would gather for a banquet of fine foods and wines. The settlers enjoyed gambling and played both cards and billiards for money. Horse racing and betting on the races was a favorite Sunday activity as well. After Sunday mass, the French went dancing. All settlers, rich and poor, young and old, attended the dances. **Cotillions**, waltzes, two-steps, and minuets were performed to the music of a fiddle. The French in Missouri were social people. They thoroughly enjoyed music, dancing, and telling stories. Not all children were taught to read, but all were taught to dance.

The first church was built six years after the village was founded. A small log chapel was built where the Old Cathedral stands today. This is the original location for a church designated in Laclède's plan. Sunday was considered a day of rest for slaves, except during harvest time. Some slaves earned extra income for their masters or for themselves by doing extra work on this day. Over time, the money they saved was used to buy their freedom, or the freedom of family members.

(An interesting tidbit of information: There were few stores or shops in the village. Later, as the village grew, the people bought items in large open-air markets. The market became a place for visiting friends and exchanging news as well as shopping.)

ST. LOUIS GROWS

Thus, St. Louis grew from a small trading post with a few families to a frontier village. By 1773, there were 637 people living in St. Louis. For many years to come, the fur trade would continue to be the major business of Upper Louisiana, and St. Louis would be at the center of that trade.

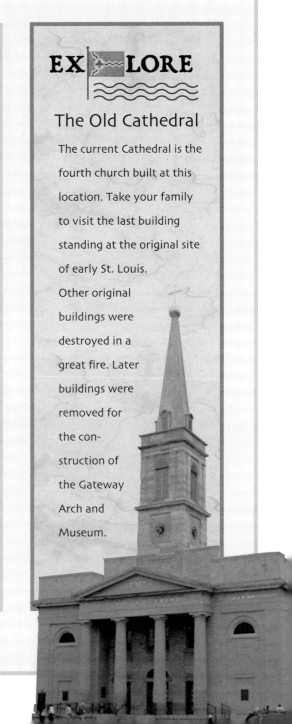

EX LORE

The Old Cathedral

The current Cathedral is the fourth church built at this location. Take your family to visit the last building standing at the original site of early St. Louis. Other original buildings were destroyed in a great fire. Later buildings were removed for the construction of the Gateway Arch and Museum.

THREE FLAGS CEREMONY

CHAPTER SIX

UNDER NEW LEADERSHIP
THE LOUISIANA PURCHASE

Imagine you are a French child born in St. Louis. You speak French, as do your parents and neighbors. You see yourself as French and live your life in a French manner. Suddenly, you learn that St. Louis is now a part of the United States of America. People who have different customs and speak a different language will settle in your neighborhood. They will bring new laws and new attitudes. The French flag is raised one last time and you cheer. You wonder how your life will change.

ST. LOUIS BECOMES SPANISH TERRITORY

Our story continues in Europe. France and Spain had become **allies**; Louis XV, the King of France, and Charles III, the King of Spain, were cousins. In 1763, after the French and Indian War, Louis XV made a treaty with his cousin, Charles III, and gave Spain the territory known as Louisiana, including the city of New Orleans. Charles III wanted to protect Spanish settlements, including Mexico, Texas, and Florida, from England.

St. Louis would now serve as an outpost of the Spanish empire. Using the boundary of the Arkansas River, Spain divided Louisiana into Upper and Lower Louisiana. A lieutenant-governor, located in St. Louis, would administer Upper Louisiana. Upper Louisiana was divided into districts: the St. Louis District was the region between the Meramec and the Missouri rivers.

The first Spanish lieutenant-governor, Don Pedro Piernas, arrived at St. Louis, the capital of Upper Louisiana, in 1770. The French commandant, St. Ange De Bellerive, formally transferred his authority to Don Pedro Piernas. The new lieutenant-governor found conditions in St. Louis to be a little unruly and the citizens in need of some discipline. St. Louis was a **frontier** village. Several problems existed reflecting this fact. Some of the new laws included the following:

- Citizens could not give alcohol to the Native Americans.
- Citizens could not spread rumors (it disturbed the public peace).

- Citizens could not leave their homes without carrying a weapon for protection.
- Citizens could not race horses or horse-drawn carts through the streets.
- Citizens could not leave their carts and plows in the streets.
- Citizens were to assemble in a protected place in case of an attack.
- Citizens needed to make wills (people died suddenly in those days).

The **customs** in St. Louis remained essentially French and unchanged under the new Spanish government. Piernas quickly learned to accept the French way of doing things. His new government recognized all existing land titles and assumed the job of granting land to settlers. He urged the French to build a log cabin church on the lot set aside for it in Laclède's plan. There were no juries or lawyers in St. Louis, and the new lieutenant-governor served as the chief legal justice for the area. Complaints and civil suits were decided by Don Pedro Piernas (murders and other major crimes were very rare). Some disputes between citizens were brought before a panel of leading citizens for their advice. Don Pedro Piernas imposed no taxes on the people of St. Louis. When the government needed funding, citizens were asked to make contributions.

One law ignored by the French stated that citizens could not keep Native Americans as slaves. Records from 1770 show that 68 Indians were held as slaves in St. Louis. Even after it was made illegal, slave owners kept their Indians slaves and any children born to them. Don Piernas did not enforce the laws freeing Indian

Trespassing Goats

The French brought plants and animals to St. Louis. Goats came with the settlers. Stockades were built around each lot to keep animals, wild and domestic, out of the gardens. Goats were notorious for eating all vegetation within their reach. If a goat managed to get into a garden, it would eat everything in sight. Goats could also injure people if provoked. One law stated that if a citizen caught a stray goat in his garden or if the animal injured a settler, the goat could be shot and the shooter would not be held responsible.

slaves, and the practice of owning African slaves remained legal.

FUR TRADE UNDER SPANISH LAW

The Spanish authorities recognized at once the importance of the fur trade in St. Louis. British fur traders, operating from Canada, **poached** furs and competed with St. Louis' **merchants**. Access to the Missouri River had to be defended at all costs. English traders were not permitted in Upper and Lower Louisiana. Spanish traders were forbidden to trap east of the Mississippi River in English-owned territories. Fur traders would now be licensed and their activities supervised by the government.

Under Spanish rule, friendly relationships with the Native Americans were a high priority. From the beginning, the Spanish government recognized Indian claims to villages, tribal lands, and hunting territories. The Spanish government understood that gift giving and trade were important aspects of Indian culture. Don Pedro Piernas issued laws declaring that Indians were to receive just prices for their furs and their tribal leaders were to be awarded annual gifts. The Spanish government allowed any settler with a proper **license** to trade with the Indians. This encouraged many small traders to enter into business.

EFFECTS OF FUR TRADE ON INDIANS

Before the Europeans came to North America, furs were not so greatly prized by the Native people because fur-bearing animals were so plentiful. But the French wanted furs to send to the European clothing industry, and Indians increasingly wanted European trade goods. Guns, knives, and ammunition

Flatboats

French voyageurs built several types of boats to use on the river. The flatboat was really just a raft. A simple shed was built at the stern of the craft to shelter passengers and cargo. Animals traveled on the open deck. A flatboat could be 50 feet long. Flatboats carried large loads and floated easily downstream, propelled by the current and the activity of oarsmen. The flatboat was crudely constructed, and it was broken apart and sold for lumber at the end of a trip.

made hunting easier and provided a strategic advantage in war with tribes who used weapons made of stone and wood. Once they acquired European guns, however, Native Americans became dependent on traders for a their supply of powder, flint, and lead balls. Indians also prized the paints, cloth, ribbons, yarn, beads, blankets, and cookware that they received from traders, which were **novel** to the goods made from their own hands. French trade goods soon became necessary for survival, and the Indians of Missouri became dependent on the French fur trade.

Tribes changed their migrations so that their paths would now cross those of the French traders. Native Americans now spent more and more time seeking furs. Soon, the over-hunting of fur-bearing animals diminished their numbers in traditional hunting territories. This need for the European products that they could not produce themselves also increased tensions between different tribes.

In addition, tribes east of the Appalachian Mountains were displaced by the English colonists. They resettled west of the Mississippi River. The English wanted to take the American Indian ancestral land for their own. They viewed Indians as inferior beings, ignored claims to their hunting grounds, and fought constantly to eliminate the Native population. As the displaced tribes came into the Louisiana territories, they competed for the same resources with the local tribes.

Unlike the English settlers, the French were few in number and didn't want as much land for settlements. The French left Indians undisturbed to hunt on their

Keelboats

Keelboats were shallow, covered boats with rounded hulls in the front and back. Keelboats could be 70 feet long. Unlike the flatboat, the keelboat's narrow hull had less drag in the water allowing it to travel both upstream and downstream. For power, the boat relied on a crew of men who walked along the riverbank pulling a rope attached to the boat. This procedure was called cordelling. At other times, the crew used long poles that touched the river bottom to push the keelboat against the current.

ancient grounds and to gather furs for trade. These French traders moved freely about an area too large to be patrolled by Spanish officials. Some Frenchmen joined tribes and became permanent residents of Indian villages.

THE BOY BECOMES AN INFLUENTIAL MAN

Auguste Chouteau grew into a remarkable man. He was active in assisting Pierre Laclède in the fur-trading business and bought Laclède's home and land after his stepfather's death. The land included a mill, a small stream that powered the mill, and a pond. Chouteau also bought all the slaves previously owned by Laclède. He bought the fur-trading company and eventually paid off Laclède's debts to Antoine Maxtent. Auguste Chouteau was an active and successful trader and the leader of the French **aristocracy** in St. Louis. At 37, Chouteau married Marie Térèse Cerré, who was 17 years old. (See replicas of their wedding clothes at the Missouri History Museum.) They had nine children. During his life, he was known as the first citizen of St. Louis and the wealthiest man in Upper Louisiana.

Chouteau was fascinated with Native American culture. For more than 20 years he traveled west, living for months at a time with tribes, including the Osage. Chouteau learned to speak the Osage language fluently, attended tribal ceremonies, and gave generous gifts to their chiefs. Chouteau even became an Osage blood brother. In return, the Osage trusted and respected him. Auguste Chouteau obtained a monopoly of the Osage fur trade from 1794 to 1802, buying thousands of furs from the tribe. The Osage became the wealthiest tribe in the area by supplying more hides and furs to traders than did any other tribe. Their hunting territory stretched from the Missouri River to south of the Arkansas River and from the Great Plains eastward almost to the Mississippi.

THE AMERICAN REVOLUTION

From the 1600s to the 1800s, people of English heritage settled on the eastern seaboard of North America. After the French and Indian War, the newly crowned King George III of England was challenged to make the colonies more stable. English Americans were in conflict with Indians over land. The Proclamation of 1763 sought to limit these conflicts. This Proclamation prohibited any English settlement west of the Appalachian Mountains, leaving that land for the Native Americans.

Daniel Boone was one of many settlers who ignored the Proclamation of 1763. In March 1775, Boone discovered the Cumberland Gap, a natural mountain pass through the Appalachian Mountains to lands in present-day Kentucky. In spite of repeated attacks by Indians, who were protecting their hunting territory, Boone and these settlers built the Wilderness Road. This road became the primary route to the West, running from eastern Virginia over the Appalachian Mountains to the interior of Kentucky.

King George III had another challenge. England was in debt. The king believed

Auguste Chouteau was a leading man of business and one of the most important citizens of early St. Louis. He was a successful merchant and land speculator and the head of extensive lead-mining operations. Chouteau held many public positions: trustee of the village of St. Louis, the president of the Bank of Missouri, a judge, and a colonel in the militia. A street in St. Louis and an island in the Mississippi River near the Chain of Rocks Bridge are named after Chouteau.

that the colonies should help pay off the debt. He **levied** taxes on many common goods imported to the colonies and important to the colonists. This made the colonists angry. The colonists argued that only their colonial assemblies, and not British Parliament, could levy taxes on them. Their slogan, "no taxation without representation," meant that they wanted to have a voice in their government.

The English colonists, who were now known as "Americans," decided to fight for their independence. The official Declaration of Independence from England was made on July 4, 1776. England sent an army to the colonies, and the war that followed was called the American Revolutionary War. The Spanish and French, at war against the English in Europe, joined the side of the Americans. France entered the war in 1778, and Spain declared war on Britain in 1779.

ATTACK ON ST. LOUIS

The area across the Mississippi from St. Louis was British territory. In 1778, George Rogers Clark led American troops and captured Fort Kaskaskia. This was an important battle, as Fort Kaskaskia, just downriver from St. Louis, was the British capital of the Illinois country. Captain Fernando De Leyba was the third Spanish lieutenant-governor in charge of St. Louis. He supported the American cause and encouraged St. Louis merchants to send money and **munitions** to help Clark in his campaign against the British.

British officers were anxious to win back their territory in Illinois. They organized an Indian expedition, under the command of British Canadians, to attack and reclaim Fort Kaskaskia. This military expedition would then attack and claim the Spanish village of St. Louis. The capture of St. Louis would bring the rich fur trade of the Missouri river under the English control.

Captain Fernando De Leyba was informed about the impending attack. The citizens of St. Louis had less than two months to fortify the village. About 250 settlers dug more than a mile of trenches around the village. A tower, about 30 feet in diameter and 35 feet in height, was built west of the St. Louis and was situated on a hill. The tower was named Fort San Carlos, after Spanish King Carlos III. Cannons were mounted in the tower and at prominent points around the perimeter of the St. Louis. Soldiers from Ste. Genevieve and hunters from the Meramec River were called to help. Within five days, these 150 reinforcements arrived to protect St. Louis.

On May 28, 1780, St. Louis was attacked. It is estimated that Captain De Leyba had only 350 men defending St. Louis against a force of 1,000 Indian warriors. Still, the small group of defenders used their cannons to great effect. In what was to be known as "L' Année du Grand Coup," the French and Spanish fired at the attackers from the trenches with muskets and from Fort San Carlos with cannons. The Indians were very afraid of the cannon fire and did not advance. Instead, they killed or wounded 28 settlers caught beyond the trenches. After two hours, they retreated, taking 25 captives with them. (An interesting tidbit of

See the historical marker on the east side of the Marriott Pavilion hotel at the corner of Broadway and Market streets. It contains information on the battle and an illustration of Fort San Carlos. You can follow the red lines painted on the sidewalks to explore more sites along the walking tour of downtown St. Louis.

information: One of the men to die that morning was Jean Marie Cardinal. He was a trader who brought his Pawnee wife to live with him in St. Louis. Cardinal Avenue in St. Louis is named in his honor.) Captain Fernando De Leyba was honored by Spain for saving St. Louis from capture. Under the direction of Auguste Chouteau, a nine-foot tall stockade was added to Fort Carlos to fortify the village against future attacks.

In the winter of 1781, a unit of soldiers from St. Louis and Cahokia, along with their Indian allies, traveled north to St. Joseph, Michigan. Their goal was to destroy supplies of arms stored by the British. It was feared that these sup-

Fort San Carlos

L'Année

The French had a custom of naming a year as a way to remember the major event. Early St. Louis history included:

1780   L'Année du Grand Coup
Year of the Great Battle

1785   L'Année des Grandes Eaux
Year of the Great Waters or Flood

1787   L'Année des Dix Battaux
Year of the Ten Boats

1797 L'Année des Galeres or Galleys
Year of boats filled with soldiers to protect St. Louis from British attack

1800 L'Année du Grand Hiver
Year of the Great Cold

1801 L'Année de la Picote
Year of the Smallpox

In the 1787, the "Year of the Ten Boats," river pirates were a major problem. The pirates hid along the banks of the Mississippi and attacked river traffic. They stole cargo and held people hostage. Soldiers patrolled the river on 10 boats and the pirates, called "river rats," were successfully driven away.

plies would be used to mount another attack against St. Louis in the spring. They surprised the British soldiers standing guard and succeeded in capturing and destroying the supplies. The triumphant party returned back safely to St. Louis in a blizzard.

By defeating the English attack in 1780, the people of St. Louis gave valuable assistance to the American Revolution. British forces never gained access to the Missouri River. If the British had succeeded in capturing St. Louis, it is possible that they would have claimed the Louisiana Territory and taken it over from Spain. Instead, the western boundary of the United States of America was drawn at the eastern edge of the Mississippi, rather than the Appalachian Mountains.

MORE PEOPLE COME TO ST. LOUIS

The United States of America replaced England as St. Louis' neighbor in 1783. The newly formed American government began to **debate** the future of slavery in the United States. It was decided to allow slavery south of the Ohio River. Slavery was made illegal north of the Ohio River. This area which included present-day Indiana, Illinois, and Ohio, was called the "Northwest Territory." Many settlers from the area moved across the river to St. Louis to keep their slaves. Some Americans moved west to avoid conflicts with Indians. Settlers were moving into Indian territory in record numbers, and the Indians were fighting back.

Spain adopted a policy of encouraging Americans to move to the sparsely settled territory. The Spanish wanted to protect Louisiana from British invasion.

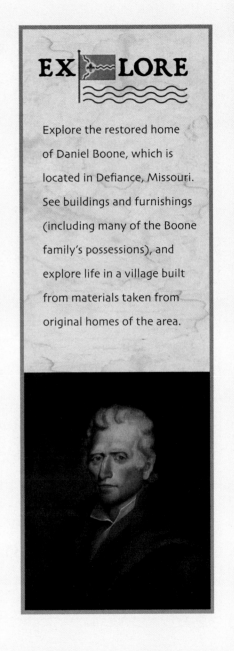

EX LORE

Explore the restored home of Daniel Boone, which is located in Defiance, Missouri. See buildings and furnishings (including many of the Boone family's possessions), and explore life in a village built from materials taken from original homes of the area.

POPULATION OF ST. LOUIS

YEAR	NUMBER OF RESIDENTS
1770	500
1773	637
1780	800
1795	1,316
1800	2,447

Land was granted free and no taxes were levied. Daniel Boone had lost most of his land in Kentucky after the Revolutionary War. The government did not accept his land claims. Boone accepted Spain's invitation to move to Louisiana and was granted a large tract of land in St. Charles county.

SPANISH TO FRENCH TO AMERICAN

In 1800, following another war in Europe, Spain returned Louisiana to France. For a short time, St. Louis was a French territory once more. Spanish officials remained in charge of Louisiana. In 1795, the Americans had negotiated the "right to deposit" their trade goods to the port of New Orleans. The city of New Orleans controlled the flow of boats traveling up and down the great Mississippi River. Americans relied on the free navigation of the river to export their goods to Europe. Although the treaty had expired in 1789, Spain allowed the continued use of the port of New Orleans by American boat traffic. But in 1802, New Orleans was closed by the Spanish to American trade. The closing of the port of New Orleans meant that Americans had lost the cheapest way to bring their goods to distant markets. This decision by Spain would bring financial disaster to the United States.

President Thomas Jefferson sent James Monroe, the future president, to Paris to negotiate the purchase of New Orleans for $2 million dollars. The response from Napoleon, the ruler of France, astonished the Americans. Napoleon offered to sell all of Louisiana. There were many reasons why

(continued on page 92)

Revolution in France and in the West Indies.

French explorers landed on the island of Hispaniola in 1625. They fought with the Spanish and eventually seized the west part of the island. The French named their part of the island St. Dominigue. They turned it into the richest colony in the world. St. Domingue produced sugar, coffee, indigo, and cotton for French markets. More sugar and coffee was grown here than in any other place in the world. France brought thousands of Africans to work in the sugar cane fields or to be sent to be sold in the slave market in New Orleans.

The spirit of freedom swept Europe after the American Revolution. The French Revolution began in 1789. Driven by the ideas of "liberty, equality, and fraternity," the French revolutionaries beheaded King Louis XVI in 1793. The newly democratic country experimented with several forms of government until Napoleon Bonaparte seized power in 1799.

On St. Domingue, slaves were ruled by a small French aristocracy of planters, merchants, and officials. Mulattoes, the children of white masters and African slaves, rebelled against this aristocracy. The mulattoes had no political freedom and wanted their own liberty and equality. Their call to freedom was heard in the slave community, which made up 85 percent of the population of St. Domingue. The slaves revolted against the aristocracy and burnt the sugar plantations, killing their masters, overseers, and other whites. England and Spain decided to take advantage of the turmoil on the island by sending troops to try and win control of St. Domingue.

The French organized an army of slaves to fight the English and Spanish. One of the black generals was Toussaint L'Ouverture. His army defeated the English first and then the Spanish. By 1793, the rebel slaves controlled the entire island and put an end to slavery on Hispaniola.

St. Domingue remained a French colony, but L'Ouverture did not want to give the island back to France. In 1796, he issued a constitution for St. Domingue and declared himself governor for life.

In 1801, Napoleon sent 82,000 troops, commanded by his brother-in-law, Charles Leclerc, to restore French rule. After two years of war, neither the slaves or the French could win. Leclerc captured L'Ouverture and sent him to France. L'Ouverture died later that year, and Jacques Dessalines emerged as the new leader of the slave rebellion. During the conflict, hundreds of French soldiers died of yellow fever, including Leclerc.

On January 1, 1804, Dessalines declared St. Domingue a free republic. The newly established nation was given the name "Haiti." The name Haiti comes from a Native word "ayiti," which means the land of mountains. Haiti joined the United States as the second independent nation in the western hemisphere.

A Bargain

The French territory of Louisiana included portions or the entire area of present-day Arkansas, Missouri, Iowa, Minnesota, North Dakota, South Dakota, Nebraska, New Mexico, Oklahoma, Kansas, Montana, Wyoming, Colorado, and Louisiana. The Louisiana Territory also included portions of southern Manitoba, southern Saskatchewan, and southern Alberta in Canada. The land included in the Louisiana Purchase comprises 23.3 percent of total current U.S. land. In 1803, the U.S. government purchased all this land from France for only $15 million dollars. In today's dollars that would be $184 million.

Napoleon decided to give up Louisiana. The cost of fighting a slave rebellion in St. Dominigue (now Haiti) had been enormously expensive for France. Napoleon was worried that slaves living in Louisiana would rebel, inspired by the successful Haitians. France needed money to engage in warfare in Europe. It was too expensive to manage the affairs of Louisiana. Selling Louisiana to the Americans would keep the land safe from British conquest.

President Jefferson seized the opportunity. In 1803, the American treasury paid $15 million for the Louisiana Purchase (about 4 cents per acre). The territory of the United States doubled in size. Its borders now reached from the Atlantic Ocean to the Rocky Mountains. St. Louis had become a vital part of the United States of America.

Spanish Flag

French Flag

U. S. A. Flag

THE DAY OF THREE FLAGS: MARCH 9-10, 1804

The United States took formal possession of Louisiana Territory in New Orleans on December 20, 1803. On March 10, 1804, a ceremony was conducted in St. Louis to transfer ownership of the Upper Louisiana territory from Spain to France to the United States. Captain Amos Stoddard and Meriwether Lewis represented the President and the United States. Lewis was in St. Louis gathering supplies for the Corps of Discovery expedition. The expedition was to travel the length of the Missouri River to explore this newly acquired territory.

The Spanish flag was lowered for the last time. The French people of St. Louis believed Spain had provided a fair and just system of government for them and were sad. Then the flag of France was raised in a **symbolic** gesture, representing the brief return of Louisiana to France. The people rejoiced (illustrated on page 78). For 24 hours, the ceremony was stopped and the French flag flew over St. Louis once again. The next day, the French flag was lowered and the flag of the United States of America rose in its place. Forty years after the founding of St. Louis (almost to the day) by French fur traders, St. Louis joined the United States of America. It marked the last time the French flag flew on the North American continent.

This was what was happening in St. Louis in 1804. It was the ending of one era and a beginning of another. Over time, St. Louis changed from a small French village to a very important American city in our country's history. St. Louis would soon become the major frontier village supplying goods and services to Americans as they moved westward. There would be many more exciting times ahead for St. Louis and the people who lived there.

Explore the Old Courthouse located near the Gateway Arch. See a model of a flatboat and keelboat. Notice the tools, weapons, and household items used by both the French and the Native Americans. Look for the dioramas of various scenes of St. Louis throughout the city's early years. Can you find the scene showing the ceremony of the Day of Three Flags? Go to the Jefferson National Expansion Memorial, an incredible museum under the Gateway Arch, to learn more about the westward expansion of our country and how St. Louis played a major role.

GLOSSARY

A

acclimate to adapt to new climate, conditions, or surroundings

allies groups on the same side by agreement in a battle or dispute

ambitious having a strong drive for success

ancestor person from whom one who is descended, usually a great-grandfather or before

aristocracy the most powerful members of a society

artifacts items created by humans in the past that exist to this day

awl a tool used to punch holes

Aztec Indian people in Mexico whose empire was conquered by the Spaniards in 1519

B

barter the exchange of goods and services without money

bluff a high, steep bank having a prominent and almost vertical front, often found along the edge of a river valley

British the people of England and Great Britain

breeches trousers ending just below the knees

C

C.E. (Common Era) time beginning with year 1 (used to be referred to as A.D. for Anno Domini, Latin for "in the year of our Lord" in Christian terms. Time before the year 1 is referred to as B.C.E. - Before Common Era.

calico a coarse fabric made from unbleached cotton printed with a small repeated design of florals or leaves

camouflage to conceal the identity of something by modifying its appearance, to disguise, to blend into the surrounding environment

civilization an advanced society, often having laws, science, art, and sometimes written language in their culture

clan a group of people sharing common ancestry

classification grouping together of similar or related things

colony people living in a new territory but retaining ties with their former country

colonist one who lives in a colony but still remains a citizen of the original country; the original country is sometimes called "the motherland"

confluence a flowing or coming together

conquistador a Spanish soldier who participated in the conquest of the New World in the 16th century

cotillion a lively dance originating in France in the 18th century

coureur-de-bois trader or trapper

Crusades Christian military expeditions of the 11th through 13th centuries to drive Muslims from the Middle Eastern Holy Land

cultivation preparing ground, planting seeds, caring for and harvesting of crops

culture/cutural heritage development of a particular people or nation at a given time; cultural heritage including its customs, art, music, architecture, religion, tools, habits, traditions

custom an accepted practice of long standing

D

debate discuss a given subject by considering opposed arguments

E

ethnic relating to large groups of people grouped according to common racial, national, tribal, religious, language, or cultural background

empire a large number of different lands ruled over by one authority, often a monarch or king.

excavation the systematic digging and recording of an archaeological site

expedition a journey for a particular purpose, such as exploration

export send goods or services out of the country to sell

extinction the total disappearance of an animal or plant that once existed but now cannot be found alive anywhere on earth.

F

famine widespread starvation

fort a strong place used for protection and most often occupied by troops; many have towers and stockade fences or ditches surrounding the buildings

frontier a wilderness at the edge of settlements

G

gourd the fruit of a vine-bearing plant such as squash

granary storehouse for grain

grid a pattern of lines laid out at right angles to each other

H

hemp a plant with tough fiber used to make rope and clothing

hereditary passed from generation to generation (such as genes or titles)

I

Ice Age the period of time when the northern hemisphere was covered with glaciers

immigrant a person who leaves one country to settle permanently in another

immunity a condition of being able to resist particular diseases by the body's building up of antibodies (microorganisms that fight it off)

impetuousity impulsive violence and force

import to bring items into a place from another place

J

Jesuit a member of a Roman Catholic religious order, the Society of Jesus

K

keel a projection along the bottom of a boat running from stern to bow, which prevents side-slipping and helps the craft maintain straight movement

L

leggings coverings made of skin that extend from just above the knees to the ankles

levy to collect money imposed on a person or property

license a legal document giving official permission to do something

loincloth a cloth worn around the waist that covers the hip region; often the only piece of clothing worn in warm climates

M

Meramec an Algonquian word; meaning "mer" meaning ugly and "amec" a fish; refers to a catfish

merchant someone who makes a living by buying and selling things for a profit

mica a colored or transparent mineral that easily separates into thin sheets or leaves

metropolitan area including a large city and its surrounding communities (towns, villages)

migrate move from one area to live in another, sometimes depending on seasons and climate changes

mill building made for grinding grain from wheat into flour; also called "gristmill"

mission a place where Christianity is being preached for the first time

missionaries people sent by a religious organization to other parts of the world to share their beliefs

monopoly the exclusive right to carry on a particular business or trade with no competition

munitions (from the French for material) military supplies such as weapons and ammunition

N

network an interconnected system of geographic features such as rivers

nomadic roaming about from one place to another, having no one set home

notorious having a bad reputation

novel new, fresh, unusual, of a kind not seen before

O

obsidian glasslike stone from volcanoes

P

persimmon orange or yellowish fruit with one to 10 seeds, to be eaten only when fully ripe

plaza a Spanish word which describes an open public space in the center of town

Polo, Marco Italian explorer and author who made numerous trips to China between 1275 and 1292 and returned to Europe to write of his journeys

poach hunt illegally

portage the carrying of a canoe

over land from one water body to another, from the French "to carry"

prehistoric before written history, "pre" meaning "before," "history" meaning "record of important past events"

privilege a special benefit not enjoyed by all

prosperity success, good fortune, wealth

R

revere to regard with great awe and devotion

ritual ceremonial behavior in which the members of a group or community regularly engage, a traditional cultural practice

S

sickle a tool with a long handle and long, slightly curved blade used to cut grass or grains

smallpox a highly contagious, often fatal disease with symptoms that include high fever and scar-

producing blisters

status rank or position in social standing

stockade strong posts stuck upright in the ground to serve as a protective fence

swaddle to wrap an infant tightly in skins or cloth

symbolic using a symbol or an object to stand for a greater idea; serving as a visible representation for something abstract

T

technology the development and application of tools, machines, materials and processes that help to solve problems

thatch a roof covering of straw or reeds

tributary a river that does not reach the sea, but joins another river and increases the volume of the receiving river

V

vessel a hollow container for holding something, such as a cup,

bowl, pitcher, bottle, or pot

voyageur-de-bois a man who transports trade goods by boat

U

Upper Louisiana the northern portion of the Louisiana Territory containing present-day Missouri

W

wigwam a dome-shaped hut made of woven sticks and grasses, made by Native Americans to use for homes

watershed all the land and tributaries draining to a body of water such as a river

western hemisphere the half of the Earth that includes North and South America and the nearby islands

Y

yellow fever a disease caused by a virus and spread by mosquitoes, with symptoms that include muscle pain, high fever, vomiting, bleeding, and sometimes death

APPENDIX

Best, Biggest, First in St. Louis

BUILDINGS AND STRUCTURES

The Gateway Arch Largest monument in the United States

The Cathedral Basilica of Saint Louis One of the greatest churches of Christendom. Has world's greatest and largest collection of mosaic art, while the main dome is the largest mosaic anywhere, the only major display that carried out a pre-established plan, and the only one completed within the lifetime of one man (70 years); 83,000 square feet of mosaics

Old Courthouse The dome was the first cast iron dome of its kind in the U. S. and weighs 128 tons. Charles Wimar murals inside were the first west of the Mississippi

Olympic Stadium, Francis Field First concrete stadium in the United States

Federal Reserve Bank in St. Louis Handles all the postal money orders for the entire nation

Barr Company First department store ever created, 1870

Union Station The largest single-use restoration project in the nation

Wainwright Building First building in the world to incorporate modern skyscraper construction; designed by Louis Sullivan, completed in 1892

First African Baptist Church The first black Protestant congregation west of the Mississippi, founded by John Berry Meachum

North Grand Water Tower Tallest Corinthian column in the world

PARKS, MUSEUMS, ATTRACTIONS

Climatron at Shaw's Garden Largest greenhouse and oldest still used; first commercially successful geodesic dome

Forest Park One of largest parks in the nation (7th largest)

Museum of Western Expansion Largest museum of the National Park System (under the Arch); 42,000 square feet of floor space

Muny Opera Largest outdoor theater in U. S.

Mastodon State Park Only site where mastodon bones and early people's (Clovis man) weapons have been found together, proving that they existed at the same time

CONFERENCES AND CONVENTIONS

Louisiana Purchase Exposition The only world's fair to turn a profit

Third Olympics The first American locale to host Olympics, 1904; with the World's Fair

First Peace Conference in the world Held in Festival Hall at World's Fair; 200 people from 15 nations

PRODUCTS

Hot dogs, iced tea, and ice cream cones First made popular at the 1904 World's Fair

World's largest fur market in 1910 And continues to be major fur market

Anheuser Busch Largest beer seller in the world

1897 St. Louis had the largest drugstore, wooden warehouse, hardware store, and tobacco factory in world, and the largest brewery, shoe factory, saddlery market, street car factories, and hardwood lumber market in the United States.

TRANSPORTATION

Union Station The largest rail terminal in the world in 1894, with 24 trunk lines converging and 400 passenger trains arriving and departing daily.

In 1897, world's biggest train station; 22 railroads met in the largest single-level passenger train station, 260 trains on 41 tracks; moved 100,000 people per day

First international balloon races In 1905 in the United States

First Presidential airplane ride Theodore Roosevelt with pilot Arch Hoxsey, 1910

The first ironclad boat built The St. Louis, built by James Eads; also was the first in America to sustain bombardment from a hostile battery; the first ever engaged in the naval forces of the world, during the Civil War; built at the Union Marine Works in Carondelet

Charles Lindbergh Made first flight of air mail from Chicago to St. Louis 1926; made the first solo nonstop flight across the Atlantic from New York to Paris; and changed the image of aviation from just a hobby for daredevils to an accepted mode of transportation

Wellston Loop Once was one of the busiest streetcar transfer points in the country

EDUCATION

First public kindergarten Developed by Susan Blow in the United States

St. Louis University Became the first university in a former slave state to welcome black students and faculty members, in 1944. Other presidents of leading universities in the former slave states were to condemn a recommendation of President Truman's Commission on Higher Education that called for integration 3 years later

MISCELLANEOUS

First Chamber of Commerce

Site of the confluence of the longest rivers of our country

Nation's first postal bank Located in University City

Crown Candy Kitchen Oldest soda fountain in St. Louis

Jefferson Barracks Largest U. S. military post in 1843, first parachute jump from plane, largest mobilizer point for World War II

Most volunteers from a community (The Hill) to volunteer for the service in Navy or the Marines in World War II. Wanted to prove loyalty and didn't want to fight Italian cousins so volunteered to fight the Japanese or in other European countries

Contributors to Saint Louis History

Rev. John Anderson An abolitionist who took over some of John Berry Meachum's work when he died; assisted Elijah Lovejoy

Josephine Baker Dancer, entertainer; helped French resistance during World War II

James Beckwourth Mountain man who tried to abolish slavery

Yogi Berra Hall of Fame baseball player

Ann Biddle Formed one of the first orphanages

Susan Blow Created first public kindergarten

Daniel Boone Pioneer, trail blazer, judge

William Wells Brown Former slave who became a doctor, writer, and abolitionist

Adolphus Busch Founder of Anheuser-Busch Breweries

Marie Chouteau "Mother of Saint Louis"

Auguste Chouteau Cofounder of Saint Louis

George Rogers Clark Fought British near Saint Louis area

William Clark Co-leader of Louisiana Purchase Expedition; Territorial Governor of Missouri; Superintendent of Indian Affairs, headquartered in Saint Louis

Samuel Clemens (Pen name: Mark Twain) steamboat captain, humorist, writer

Miles Davis Musician and composer

Dr. Thomas Dooley Founder of Medico (now CARE)

Captain James Eads Created armored boats, designed and created Eads Bridge

T. S. Eliot Writer and poet

Eugene Field Poet

John Frémont Explorer, trail blazer; involved in the Civil War

General Daniel Frost Civil War general involved in the skirmish in Saint Louis

Joe Garagiola Great baseball player

Ulysses S. Grant Civil War general and President

Scott Joplin Musician and composer, created ragtime music

Elizabeth Keckley Taught at Meachum's school, later became Mary Todd Lincoln's dressmaker

Pierre Laclède Cofounder of Saint Louis

Charles Lindbergh Pilot who was first to fly solo, nonstop over the Atlantic Ocean

Manuel Lisa Successful fur trader

Elijah Lovejoy Abolitionist, journalist, and editor

Annie Malone First self-made woman millionaire in U. S.; made her money in cosmetics for African-Americans

John Berry Meacham Teacher, preacher, and businessman who founded Freedom School and started the first black church in Missouri

Stan Musial Great baseball player

James Cash (J. C.) Penney Created J. C. Penney Company

Joseph Pulitzer Journalist known for flashy design and bold reporting; owner of the early *Post-Dispatch*; Pulitzer Prize named for him

Eero Saarinen Designed the Gateway Arch

Isaac Sellers Riverboat captain

Henry Shaw Contributed Missouri Botanical Garden and Tower Grove Park

William Tecumseh Sherman General and leader in Civil War

Captain Henry Shreve Steamboat captain

Louis Sullivan Architect, teacher of Frank Lloyd Wright

Cultural Institutions, Landmarks and Tourist Attractions of the St. Louis Area

Arch
11 N. 4th Street, 314-655-1700

Bellefontaine Cemetery
4947 W. Florissant Avenue, 314-381-0750

Bellerive Park
Broadway at Bates

Black World History Museum 2505
St. Louis Avenue, 314-241-7057

Butterfly House (Faust Park)
15185 Olive Boulevard,
636-530-0076

Blueberry Hill (and Walk of Fame)
6504 Delmar, 314-727-0880

Busch Stadium
Downtown, 314-421-3060

Calvary Cemetery
5239 W. Florissant, 314-381-1313

Campbell House Museum
1508 Locust, 314-421-0325

Cahokia Mounds Historic Site
Collinsville, Illinois, 618-346-5160

Cardinals Hall of Fame Museum
11 Stadium Plaza, 314-231-6340

Carondelet Historic Site
6303 Michigan Avenue,
314-481-6303

City Museum
701 North 15th Street,
314-231-2489

Creve Coeur Park and Lake
Creve Coeur, 314-615-7275

Crown Candy Kitchen
1401 St. Louis Avenue,
314-621-9650

Daniel Boone Home
1868 Highway F, 636-798-2005

**American Kennel Club
Museum of the Dog**
1721 S. Mason Road,
314-821-3647
(also called The Dog Museum)

Eads Bridge
Downtown Riverfront

**Eugene Field House
and St. Louis Toy Museum**
634 S. Broadway, 314-421-4689

Faust Historic Village
15185 Olive Street Road,
636-532-7298

Forest Park Education Center
314-367-7275

Fort Bellefontaine Historic Site
Bellefontaine Road, Riverview
314-686-0973

Fox Theatre
527 N. Grand, 314-534-1111

Golden Eagle River Museum
Bee Tree Park, 314-846-9073

Greater Ville Monument
Martin L. King Boulevard and
Sarah Avenue, 314-534-8015

**International Bowling Museum and
Hall of Fame** 111 Stadium Plaza,
314-231-6340

**Jefferson Barracks Historic County
Park**   314-544-5714 and
Powder Magazine Museum
544-4154

**Jefferson National Expansion
Memorial**
11 N. 4th Street, 314-655-1700

Lafayette Park
Lafayette and Park

Lone Elk Park
Outer Road; Highway 141
and I-44, 314-615-7275

Lewis and Clark Boat House
1050 Riverside Drive; St. Charles,

Nature Center
636-947-3199

Lewis and Clark State Historic Site
Highway 3; Hartford, Illinois,
618-251-5811

Magic House
516 S. Kirkwood Road,
314- 822-8900

Mastodon State Historic Site
Seckman Road, 636-464-2976

Missouri Botanical Garden
4344 Shaw Boulevard
314-577-9400

Missouri History Museum
Forest Park, 314-746-4599

The Muny
Forest Park, 314-361-1900

Museum of Transportation
3015 Barrett Station Road
314-965-7998

New Cathedral
4431 Lindell, 314-533-2824

Old Capital in St. Charles
230 S. Main Street, 636-946-7776

Old Cathedral
209 Walnut, 314-231-3250

Old Courthouse
11 N. 4th Street, 314-655-1700

Osage Tribal Museum
819 Grandview St.
Pawhuska, Oklahoma 74056
918-287-5441

St. Louis Art Museum
1 Fine Arts Drive, 314-721-0072

St. Louis Post-Dispatch
900 N. Tucker Boulevard,
314-340-8888

St. Louis Powell Symphony Hall
718 N. Grand Boulevard
314-533-2500

St. Louis Science Center and
Planetarium
5050 Oakland Avenue
314-289-4444

St. Louis Union Station
Market and 18th Street

St. Louis Walk of Fame
6505 Delmar, 314-727-7827

St. Louis Zoo
Wells Drive, Forest Park
314-781-0900

Scott Joplin House State Historic
Site 2658 Delmar, 314-340-5790

Soulard Farmers Market
730 Carroll, 314-622-4180

Tower Grove Park
Grand and Magnolia
314 289-5300

Ulysses S. Grant National
Historical Site
7400 Grant Road, 314-842-3298

Union Station
1820 Market Street, 314-421-6655

Wax Museum of St. Louis
Laclede's Landing, 314-241-1155

World Bird Sanctuary
185 Bald Eagle Ridge Road,
636-225-4390

RESOURCES

Bailey, Gerrick, David C. Swan, John W. Nunley, Sean Standing Bear. *The Art of the Osage*. University of
Washington Press, 2004.

Brennan, Charles and Ben Cannon. *Walking Historic Downtown St. Louis*. St. Louis: Virginia Publishing
Co., 2001.

Cahokia Mounds Museum Society. *Cahokia, City of the Sun*. 1999.

Chapman, Carl H. and Eleanor F. Chapman. *Indians and Archaeology of Missouri*.
Columbia, Missouri: University of Missouri Press, 1983.

Carpenter, Allan. *The New Enchantment of America, Missouri*. Childrens Press, 1978.

Collins, Earl A. *Missouri*. Ramfre Press, 1955.

Coyle, Elinor Martineau. *Saint Louis, Portrait of a River City*. St. Louis: The Folkstone Press, 1966.

Denny, Sidney and Ernest Schusky. *The Ancient Splendor of Prehistoric Cahokia*. Prairie Grove, Arkansas:
Ozark Publishing, Inc., 1997.

Faherty, William Barnaby, S. J., Ph. D. *St. Louis, A Concise History*. St. Louis: Masonry Institute of St.
Louis, 1999.

_____. *The St. Louis Portrait*. Tulsa, Oklahoma: Continental Heritage Press, 1978.

Foley, William E. *The Genesis of Missouri, From Wilderness Outpost to Statehood.* University of Missouri Press, 1989.

Ford, Barbara. St. Louis, *A Downtown America Book.* Dillon Press, 1989.

Fradin, Dennis B. *Missouri in Words and Pictures.* Chicago: Childrens Press, 1980.

Gill, McCune. *The St. Louis Story.* St. Louis: Historical Record Association, 1952.

Greene, Lorenzo J., Gary R. Kremer, Antonio F. Holland. *Missouri's Black Heritage.* Columbia, Missouri: University of Missouri Press, 1993.

Hagan, Harry M. *Saint Louis Portraits of the Past.* St. Louis: Riverside Press, 1976.

_____. *This Is Our St. Louis.* St. Louis: Knight Publishing Co., 1970.

Hakim, Joy. *A History of US. Book 1 to 3.* Oxford: Oxford University Press, 1993-1999.

Karsch, Robert F. and Gertrude D. May. *Our Home State Missouri.* State Publishing Company, 1958.

LaDoux, Rita C. *Missouri* (*Hello U. S. A.* series) Lerner Publications, 1991.

Lange, Dena and Merlin M. Ames. *St. Louis, Child of the River - Parent of the West.* St. Louis: Webster Publishing Company, 1939.

Liebert, Robert. *Osage Life and Legends*. Happy Camp, CA: Naturegraph Publishers, Inc., 1987.

Loewen, James W. *Lies My Teacher Told Me*. New York: Touchstone, 1995.

Magnan, William B. and Marcella C. Magnan. *The Streets of St. Louis*. St. Louis: Virginia Publishing Co., 1994 and 1996.

McNulty, Elizabeth, *St. Louis Then and Now*. San Diego, California: Thunder Bay Press, 2000.

Primm, James Neal. *Lion of the Valley*. St. Louis, Missouri. second edition. Boulder, Colorado: Pruett Publishing Co., 1990.

Proetz, Arthur. *I Remember You, St. Louis*. St. Louis: The Zimmerman-Petty Co., 1963.

Quigley, Martin. *St. Louis, A Fond Look Back*. St. Louis: The First National Bank in St. Louis, 1956.

Reihecky, Janet. *The Osage*. Mankato, Minnesota: Bridgestone Books, 2003.

Sanford, William R. and Carl R. Green. *Missouri, (America the Beautiful* series). Chicago: Childrens Press, 1990.

Seifert, Shirley. *The Key to St. Louis*. J. B. Lippincott Co., 1963.

Stadler, Frances Hurd. *St. Louis Day by Day*. St. Louis: The Partice Press, 1989.

Thompson, Kathleen. *Missouri, Portrait of America*. Raintree Publishers, 1986.

Wilson, Terry P. *The Osage*. New York: Chelsea House Publishers, 1988.

Wolferman, Kristie C. *The Osage in Missouri*. University of Missouri Press, 1997.

Wright, John A. *Discovering African-American St. Louis: A Guide to Historic Sites*. St. Louis: The Missouri Historical Society Press, 1994.

INDEX

Picture Credits

ABOUT THE AUTHOR

Maureen Hoessle, better known as Marty, grew up in south St. Louis and has lived in the St. Louis area most of her life. She received a Masters Degree in Education from Washington University and has worked in the field of education for more than 20 years. Marty has spent the majority of her career at Community School, where she currently is teaching third grade. She was honored in 2004 with the Teacher of Distinction Award, given by the Independent Schools of St. Louis as well as the Emerson Excellence in Education Award. For the last three years, she has served on the Instruction Committee of the National Council of Social Studies. While developing her social studies curriculum, she discovered that no current children's books were available on the subject of early St. Louis; this inspired her to write *Under Three Flags*. You may easily run into her one day rollerblading in Forest Park, touring the Zoo, hiking a nature trail, viewing the latest museum exhibit, or enjoying a local musical, theatrical, or dance venue.

ABOUT THE ILLUSTRATOR

Kim Mulkey Young is an award-winning illustrator. This is the twenty-first book that she has illustrated for children, including the *Time Surfer* series for Bantam Books, *Let's Play Peek-a-Boo* for Western Publishing, and *The Joys of Christmas* by Macmillan Publishing; and her first as a book designer for Virginia Publishing. During her career, Kim has illustrated for magazines such as *Highlights for Children*, *Scholastic Magazine* and *Weekly Reader*. Her clients have also included many notable publishers of educational material for children. After growing up in various places and cultures as the daughter of an Air Force pilot, Kim attended Mount Holyoke College and the Paier College of Art. Most recently, she immersed herself in learning computer graphics and design at Forest Park Community College. When not drawing and painting, Kim enjoys walking, home decorating, watching movies and dancing with her husband Bryan. She also enjoys the company of her three-pound dog, Tazmarelda Toodle.